living in tiny HOMES

Marion Hellweg

living in tiny HOMES

Big Ideas for Small Spaces

PRESTEL

Munich • London • New York

Just one
WORD

> "Happiness doesn't need a lot of space

Marion Hellweg

As a child, I always loved camping. The feeling of freedom and being close to nature combined with the knowledge that you don't need a lot to be happy was simply magical. This enthusiasm for the great outdoors has not changed to this day – I still like to stay in a tent and go camping – even if a comfortable bed might seem rather more tempting than a blow-up mattress. Sometimes I simply pack everything I need into a large rucksack and set off to explore the world. And I really do enjoy not having so many things in my possession because, if I'm honest, I have far too much clutter around me in everyday life as it is. By that I mean things that I don't really need but that I have not rid myself of, so they still take up unnecessary space in drawers, cupboards and corners at home.

From time to time I feel a great longing for reduction, for minimization, for going back to basics. What if I moved into a smaller apartment and got rid of everything that is not essential? What if I were able to focus only on what is really necessary? A clear and tidy stage to live on, so to speak, without too many side scenes? In such moments I realize that it is not the possession of things that makes me truly happy, but that letting go does. Because the less I own, the freer I am to perceive life in all its forms and to concentrate on what happiness is all about. ■

Contents

HOME**VIEW**

014 JUST SIMPLIFY YOUR LIFE
A sustainable tiny home in Sydney

048 FLEXIBLE LIVING
A cool miniature house in South Africa

064 NEW IN NEW YORK
A tiny refuge in West Village

094 UP CLOSE TO NATURE
A family refuge in Copenhagen

128 BIG LIFE, SMALL SPACE
A stylish apartment in Cape Town

146 LOFT-STYLE LIVING
A small old apartment in Amsterdam

160 A HOME WITH A SOUL
A loft apartment in Paris

190 CHILL OUT IN NATURE
A holiday home in northern Germany

INTER**VIEW**

030 EACH PROJECT IS A PUZZLE
The INT2architecture architect duo

078 THE MAN FOR URBAN FLAIR
Architect Michael K. Chen

112 YOU HAVE TO THINK OUTSIDE THE BOX
Architect Nicholas Gurney

142 EACH PIECE DOES LOTS MORE
The kaschkasch designer duo

176 PLUS ONE MORE ROOM, PLEASE
The Danish 'add a room' enterprise

OVER**VIEW**

024 NEATLY STORED
Everything sorted and stashed away

042 A WELL-PLANNED BATHROOM
Modern baths on a small footprint

058 EVERYTHING IS FOLDABLE
Functional and versatile furniture

072 SMART KITCHENS
Innovative modules and cooking niches

084 CLEVER ROOM SOLUTIONS
Individually planned room concepts

104 NEAT AND TIDY HALLWAY
Versatile interiors for narrow spaces

120 VALUABLE STORAGE SPACE
Ideas for every corner at home

136 FLEXIBLE & PORTABLE
Small furniture that stays on the move

152 NICELY SORTED CLOTHES
From built-in wardrobe to clothes rail

168 ON THE WALL
Optimal use of vertical areas

182 SLEEPING LIKE A DREAM
Small but comfortable: the bedroom

SELECTED**VIEW**

198 INSIGHTS INTO TINY HOUSES
Eight small houses to buy or rent

---

218 Suppliers, manufacturers & information

220 About the authors

221 Thanks

223 Picture credits

" Making the most of
every corner is an art

LIVING IN A FEW SQUARE METRES

> *Small living space, great quality of life*

How would we like to live in the future? Or to put it another way: how much and what kind of space do we really need to live? It's a topic that more and more people are trying to come to grips with. On the one hand, living space is becoming ever more expensive and scarce. And on the other hand, new ways of thinking are clearly gaining some ground, a conscious attempt to live in a way that is more aware, more climate-friendly and environmentally conscious and more mindful – and to return to a simpler, more basic existence.

Downsizing is a term that is often used to describe living on a smaller footprint. What is meant is a downsizing of our needs, far removed from omnipresent consumerism; a reduction in everyday objects and interior furniture and fittings. In addition, an excessive need and waste of resources can be avoided simply through living in a smaller home. If you have less space, you cannot buy as much and you will automatically use less energy.

But what really motivates people, especially with a view to the future, to move into a tiny home? Is it the maxim that 'less is more'? Or are factors other than those already mentioned even greater inducements for a reduction in practical terms? And are minimalist, innovative living concepts also suitable for families in their everyday lives, or do they work only for singles and couples?

In this book, you will find some insightful answers to these important questions. In addition, you will discover that it is very easy to live in a much more restrained manner than before and than you might have thought possible. And you will also see that you do not have to forego your personal furnishing style and preferences.

In 1997, the English architect Sarah Susanka wrote her book *The Not So Big House – A Blueprint for the Way We Really Live*. In it, she explained that the number of square metres has almost nothing to do with the feeling of being at home. She propagated the move away from living on a large scale and launched the guiding principle of 'think smaller', which has inspired the Tiny House Movement in the United States since it began in the 1990s.

Since then, mini refuges have been steadily gaining a firm place among the most popular living trends. A growing number of tiny house manufacturers produce homes on wheels and for fixed locations. In addition, many architects have specialized in the planning of tiny apartments and offer individualized living concepts with clever storage space solutions, especially for people in large cities.

Ultimately, you will have to decide for yourself how large your surroundings should be for you to feel comfortable. And even if you don't live in a tiny home, you are sure to find in this book cool living ideas and clever storage space solutions for more space and order within your own four walls. ■

More space, more light, more air!

Just
SIMPLIFY
YOUR LIFE

Marnie and her family don't need much to enjoy life and be happy. And what little they do need fits easily into their light-flooded Tiny Home in Sydney.

Marnie and Dan, Ella and little Frankie are happy in their 32 sq m (345 sq ft) home. They share views with us on Instagram (@_tinyhaus).

14

Light weight sofa beanbags make up the living-room seats. They serve as comfortable movie loungers or a play corner – just as needed.

After suffering a work burn-out, Marnie decided to turn her hectic life around and to declutter her home. Only what felt good and what was needed would stay. The Australian opted for less stress and more joy, swapping her old job for an independent career as a lifestyle coach. At the same time, Marnie exchanged her large, cluttered home for a little house of just 32 sq m (345 sq ft). The family constructed their new home in the garden of the old house which is now rented out. A tall fence separates the two buildings. A pent roof (also known as monopitch) protects the tiny house and its adjoining terrace. Numerous windows allow sunshine to flood the home while opening lovely views to the outdoors. A calm and relaxed atmosphere is important to the family, and that's why light colours and warm wood dominate. The colourful jumble of belongings disappears behind closed cupboard fronts

The Australian family love the outdoor life – they swim, cycle, paddle, surf and camp – and their new home opens up over its entire length to the garden. The main garden features are the pool, a fire pit and the terrace. There is also space for a shed for storing bikes, boards and other outdoor living essentials. Only what is truly important to the family was moved into the house. Marnie has no problem clearing out her surplus possessions; after all, her job is helping people lead an easier life. Before moving, Marnie went through every room in the old house and sorted things out. All the family, the parents and their daughters, parted with unnecessary clothes and toys, furniture and kitchen accessories, linen and books. Even today, Marnie occasionally goes through the cupboards and drawers and decides what is superfluous. Because with simplicity and little clutter you'll enjoy a better life. ∎

Even the smallest kitchen has room for an induction hob, oven and dishwasher – sometimes at a reduced size.

Cabinets for cleaning utensils, bags and school books are stashed away under the stairs that lead to the children's room.

Marnie's cupboards are neat and tidy. There is always sufficient space for the essentials and everything is within easy reach.

The kitchen worktop extends out to the terrace and doubles as a bar counter as the window can be flipped open.

Whether indoors or out, Marnie always sets up her workplace in pleasant surroundings where she will be undisturbed.

Clothes rails, shelves, boxes, coat hooks – everything in the kids' room is also neat and tidy.

Climbing challenge, route to the bed and storage space – the multiplex-panel staircase has many functions.

The children's accommodation extends over several levels, with space to play on one and bedrooms on the other two. The girls love their realm and the child-friendly stairs.

The table is the heart of a multi-purpose corner. It serves for dining, playing, drawing, chatting and as a desk.

The bedroom wardrobes provide plenty of space for clothes, shoes, books and luggage.

Practical: the dirty washing disappears in a basket behind a built-in folding door.

The storage space under the parents' bed easily converts into a temporary play area.

Where there's no space for bedside tables, the night-time reading material simply goes into a holder on the wall next to the bed.

Neatly STORED

What to do with all the things that tend to create chaos? Well sorted and stashed away, they can be kept under control.

Decluttering expert Marie Kondo tells us that every single item needs its own place, and if you consistently put each piece back where it belongs, keeping an orderly home will suddenly be a doddle. First of all, however, a big sorting out session is called for.

For Marie Kondo, each object should trigger feelings of happiness to earn the right to stay. You don't have to be quite that strict, but it's worth taking a very critical look at your possessions and freely chucking out.

Next it's time to sort and tidy away all the things that are allowed to stay. Some people stow everything they own in labelled containers - from their collection of watches to toothpaste. You don't necessarily have to go quite that far. It's a good idea, however, to divide large containers and compartments into smaller areas, or to contain items that easily slide around in baskets and boxes.

In drawers, for example, you can create partitions or compartments to structure the interior. On shelves and in cupboards, boxes and cases are useful aids for storing together what is the same and keeping apart what is different. What's needed every day is kept at the front, everything else can stay in the background. ∎

ALL EGGS IN ONE BASKET
There's nothing like a tidy hallway. You can sit on the bench under the small cupboard to tie your shoes, while scarves and shawls, gloves and hats are stored in the pretty baskets.

Good idea: mirror doors

STRONG GUYS Do metal shelves belong in the basement? Those days have been over since more interesting metal shelves have started hitting the market. The bonus point is that metal shelves are light in weight, yet extremely robust and, thanks to their open aspect, they're perfect for small rooms.

Mix of seagrass and metal

ATTACHED Whether in the kitchen or the children's room, the bedroom or the bathroom, S-hooks do a great job. They can be attached to anything and serve as holders for bags, baskets, belts etc.

WANDERING STAR Ladder shelves can lean anywhere and offer more storage space than you might think.

CABIN ONE

Andreas Rauch and **Simon Becker**, the two founders of Cabin One, build tiny houses with a minimalist touch.

All built-in

Cabin One builds small houses with only a few square metres of living space, yet their cabins convey a surprisingly open feeling. Of course, the area available is strictly limited, and so it needs to be used to optimal effect.

Storage space is the be-all and end-all, because even if the residents have reduced their belongings to a minimum, there will still be a large number of items that need to be accommodated. Cabin One puts its money on built-in cupboards for every free spot – cupboards, compartments and drawers are hidden in corners, under the sleeping floor and below the bench. Thanks to their plain fronts, everything looks tidy.

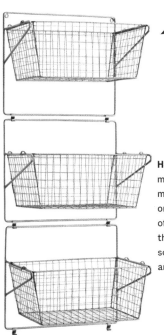

Can be extended

HIGH POLISH The metal baskets from madamstoltz.dk hang on the wall like a breath of thin air, and yet they hold anything from socks and toys to towels and craft accessories.

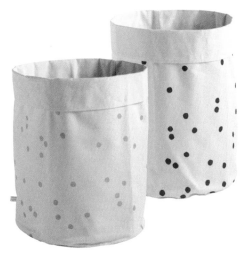

USEFUL UTENSILS Much too nice to disappear inside the wardrove – the pretty fabric baskets from lacerisesurlegateau.fr.

STACKS OF STACKS
The wooden Knagglig boxes from ikea.com can be stacked to form a proper shelf wall. But of course they also provide practical storage in cupboards and under benches, on shelves and under a raised bed.

ALWAYS TO HAND
Practical folding boxes can be stacked to form colourful towers or placed next to each other on a shelf. They're just as useful in the living room as in the children's room, and when they're not needed, they won't take up much room when folded away. These boxes are from aykasa.com.

3 COOL TIPS

The best friends of tidiness and ready
for any kind of **STORAGE** are containers
in all shapes, sizes and materials.

Baskets

Whether for a picnic or to keep things tidy, for shopping or for harvesting – baskets are universally useful. The materials from which they're made and their shapes are almost as diverse as their uses. The classics are woven from natural materials and bring an air of purity into the home. Metal baskets, on the other hand, are stylish and delicate. Fabric utensil holders can be stuffed into any corner, and felt baskets are surprisingly robust and even hold firewood. Baskets with a handle can be hung up, and square ones are perfect for newspapers and magazines.

Boxes

Boxes are straightforward. Their angular shape means they can store anything and also be stacked. Open crates can be filled higher, but those with lids keep dust away from towels, winter jackets and bed linen, for example, when stowed under the bed or on top of the wardrobe. Attractive boxes made of wood or metal can be transformed into entire shelving systems or individually attached to the wall as hanging shelves. Folding boxes made of plastic, on the other hand, bring a casual atmosphere and bright colours into the room.

Cartons

Cardboard boxes are useful not only for packaging gifts and parcels, they're also excellent keepers of order. Whether high heels or sunglasses, letters or photos, paper clips or Christmas tree decorations – smaller or more fragile items especially can safely be stored in cartons. Some are made of wood, but most cartons are cardboard. If you want to give your cardboard boxes a personal touch, paint them with pretty patterns or cover them with decorative stickers – this is also a good upcycling idea for shoe boxes, by the way.

INT2 ARCHITECTURE

EACH PROJECT IS A PUZZLE

Alexander Malinin
and **Anastasia
Sheveleva**
redecorate public
and private interiors
in and around
St Petersburg.

Light walls and wooden floors make the small room look more open. Splashes of colour ensure freshness and cheer.

We're always looking for very sophisticated solutions

You founded your INT2architecture studio in 2013. Is there one particular area in which you generally specialize?

We design houses for private customers, but we mainly design interiors. Whether it's an old country cottage or an industrial building, it's always exciting to breathe new life into the four walls in need of renovation. We love the freedom of working with our customers who bring us interesting and exciting jobs. It's so nice to see the result of our work at the end of the day and to get great feedback from the

people who live in these houses. Their response is valuable for our workflow.

With your work you win one award after another. Where does your inspiration for such excellent ideas come from?

We don't work like artists who fill a blank canvas with their ideas. Instead, we ask our customers for their wishes and specifications. We look at the rooms which already exist and try to find the best possible solution for the situation on each occasion. It's a bit like a puzzle that needs to be solved.

And in small apartments and small rooms these puzzle pieces tend to be especially tricky to fit together, aren't they? What are the main challenges?

The greatest challenge is always to find a compromise between what the customer needs and what looks attractive. In tiny homes every centimetre counts. Often it comes down to rethinking the way people live. We have to invent completely new solutions for everyday routines and for living and lifestyles in general. And in fact, this is also what we love best about designing and planning small apartments.

The lack of space always leads to completely unexpected but entirely ingenious and creative new solutions.

And do you have any useful tips to pass on to people who set up home in small houses?

Think carefully about what you really need to live your life. Only take those things with you into your tiny home that you really cannot live without. Once you have decided what you absolutely need, you'll have the starting point for planning. How can you fit your essential belongings and everything you want and need to do into the available space? ∎

Apartment № 1

This platform serves as a visual marker of the bedroom. Plus, there is plenty of storage space for all sorts of bulky items underneath.

Curtains up for the wardrobe: storage space is hidden in the partition between hallway and bedroom – accessible from both sides.

White walls and ceiling spotlights make this narrow, windowless lobby area appear much brighter.

Tiny tables work just as well as compact bedside cabinets, but they look less cumbersone.

The kitchen counter functions as a dining area as well as housing valuable storage space and even a wine rack.

Black, opaque blackboard paint turns the kitchen cupboard into a noticeboard and creativity zone.

The top cabinets extend all the way up to the ceiling. Rarely used kitchen utensils are stored at the very top.

Apartment No 1

WHO? A single woman

WHAT? Creating maximum living space in a very small footprint

FAVOURITE FEATURE? The partition walls which are thick enough to create additional storage space

One of the highlights in the bathroom is the fun themed crossword tiles on the wall.

Old army crates have been transformed into a bench. Of course they also provide practical storage space.

A projector transforms the sliding door into a home cinema screen.

Apartment No 2

WHO? A room for a teenager

WHERE? In the family apartment

WHAT? Various different functions and cool design in a small space

FAVOURITE FEATURE? The multi-functional box

The clothes cupboard very gently glides on small wheels out of its recess.

Instead of many small pieces of furniture, there are now only a few elements in this room.

Sleeping, chilling, storing – all this can be done in the multifunctional box that takes up half of the room.

The kitchen utensils and foods
are kept in self-made cupboards
and hanging shelves.

The concrete walls and ceilings were retained, and an expert took care of modern installations such as the lighting technology.

Industrial look: the designers had the welding work on the cupboards and shelves done by the car workshop around the corner.

Apartment No 3

39

The free-standing staircase is a sculptural feature and it also provides a lot of storage space.

Apartment No 3

WHO? A couple with a cat

WHAT? Turning a shell with a small footprint into a beautiful home and making as much as possible yourself

FAVOURITE FEATURE? The experience of creating the interior yourself despite little technical background knowledge

The sofa cushions sit on a platform which conceals storage space and a pull-out table.

A ladder leads to the sleeping area for overnight guests on the upper level.

Space-saving sliding doors connect and separate the rooms on the first floor from the landing.

When it's not in use, the fold-down wall-mounted desk in the reading corner is simply folded back up.

Tiles instead of a tub

DIVIDED
The tiled wall of the shower cubicle also serves as a divider from the toilet. This means there is sufficient privacy for both areas and the room can be used by two people at the same time in the early-morning rush hour.

A well-planned
BATHROOM

Wet room – no way! Modern bathrooms today are small wellness oases. This also works on the tiniest footprint.

HOMEMADE A custom-made welded base cabinet, such as this cool unit, uses all the available space to perfection. The grilles make it look nice and airy – and somehow extravagant.

On a weekday morning, the bathroom gets really busy – everyone has to shower, brush their teeth, get ready, often several people at the same time. At such times, even spacious rooms quickly reach their limits. If, on the other hand, your bathroom provides only a very limited space, this will need to be used to maximum capacity. And of course the feel-good factor shouldn't be neglected. After all, a bathroom should be more than just the sum of its functions.

Most items should be stowed away so that your eyes don't catch sight of all the little gadgets, and everything is clear and tidy. Towels and toothbrush mugs, hair dryer and scales, cleaning supplies and toilet paper – they all need a fixed place, ideally behind closed doors. This makes the bathroom look airy and spacious. There are a number of ways to create the necessary storage space. A cupboard under the washbasin, for example, offers plenty of space, as does a tall, narrow cupboard.

A ladder leaning against the wall can hold the towels and a corner shelf inside the shower the soap and shampoo. There is even free wall space for shelves or cupboards above the toilet and washbasin. ∎

OLD STAGER The String shelf is a classic. For decades it's been hanging and standing in various sizes in countless apartments all over the world. It also shows its versatility in the bathroom – plenty of storage space, a light design, plus clever options for hanging up accessories.

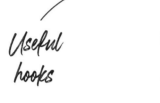

Useful hooks

ILLUSION A light shaft, a mirrored wall and glass all enlarge the bathroom.

PAOLA

Paola Bagna founded her architectural office with bases in Berlin and Empuriabrava (Spain). Her projects take her all over Europe and Africa.

Micro to maxi

An architect with Spanish roots, Paola is a true all-rounder. She will happily design the interior of a boutique hotel in Africa and next go on to give a Berlin restaurant a facelift. Her pen conjures up the look of a children's room and then sketches a company's exhibition stand. No matter what she creates, everything is always bright, clear and straightforward, with a touch of extravagance. This also applies to the micro-apartments in different parts of Berlin which Paola has converted into veritable gems. Loads of style and the joys of living in a tiny space.

REFLECTIONS Mirrors are essential in every bathroom. If placed cleverly, they will reflect the daylight that comes in through the window, making the room look brighter and airier. Here, a whole collection of mirrors is employed.

LIFT OFF Washbasins come in all shapes and sizes, so you can make the right choice for every bathroom, no matter how small. If you suspend the basin unit above the floor, the bathroom will appear more spacious.

SPACE MIRACLE Narrow, tall cabinets fit into almost any niche. Closed fronts are particularly practical as they hide the less attractive items.

DECORATIVE Ladders that lean against the wall are extremely useful. They're space-saving and you can hang towels and flannels on them to dry. This particular ladder from car-moebel.de also has a box shelf at the top.

3 COOL TIPS

Often people give little thought to the
BATHROOM. With good planning, however,
it can become the family's favourite room.

Tiles

The bigger the better. This is the motto of people who choose tiles for their small bathrooms. While small tiles and wide joints make a room seem busy and restless, reducing it visually in size, large tiles laid with narrow joints conjure up the impression of a homogeneous, uniform surface. It means that even a small bathroom looks much bigger. Those who are even stricter opt for a bathroom without tiles, using for example clay plaster on the walls and terrazzo on the floor. And mosaics? They're best used only sparingly as accents.

Shower

Bathtub or shower? Unfortunately, there is no room for both in a tiny bathroom. Generally, most people opt for a shower rather than a tub. That's good for the design of the bathroom, because a shower takes up significantly less space and so it also makes the room seem larger – especially when the floor tiles extend into the shower area and a glass partition allows light to filter through. If you don't want to do without a relaxing bath, you're best off opting for a corner bath which takes up less space.

Furniture

Tubes and pots, hot water bottles, scales and flannels – countless objects need to be stowed away in a bathroom. A small room looks more expansive when it's tidied up, which is why storage space is extremely important. All the items need to have their own place and, if possible, disappear behind doors and in drawers. No matter which furniture items you choose, if you hang them on the wall, they appear to float above the floor. This gives the whole area a certain lightness and makes every bathroom, no matter how small, appear more spacious.

Flexible
LIVING

Here today, there tomorrow. The mobile home of South Africans Khanyi and Dawn could just as easily stand in a backyard as in a green meadow.

The tiny home rises out of the meadow like a work of art. Its plain façade is made from lacquered wood, while the extravagant roof is clad in metal.

Who needs a large house when everything that is important fits a cleverly designed space of 17 sq m (183 sq ft)? Certainly not these two.

The bathroom is hidden in one of the cubes, while you will find the shower in the hallway, right in front of the bathroom door.

For the time being, Khanyi and Dawn have settled in their paradise outside Johannesburg. They love the panoramic views of the wide landscape, into which their tiny house fits like a sculpture. The couple did not want to commit themselves for long years and initially leased a meadow with a view. Who knows, maybe one day they will put their mobile home on the beach or in the city centre? The interior of the house is just as flexible as the location. The 17 sq m (183 sq ft) are real all-rounders: you shower in the hallway, eat, work and relax in the kitchen. The work area also doubles as a guest room, with a corner for laundry drying and storage space. Sleeping happens under the roof: the bed is directly under a large porthole window on a recessed second level. A ladder leads up, so narrow that it does not have any impact life on the ground floor. Thanks to the window front, which can be completely opened to the terrace, the entire mobile home is bright and flooded with light.

The kitchen base units are permanently fixed. The shelves above, on the other hand, can be rearranged as desired.

With such a garden, who wouldn't opt for the outdoor life? The open window front helps to blur the boundaries.

If friends come to visit while
it is raining, they can still be
comfortable on the patio.

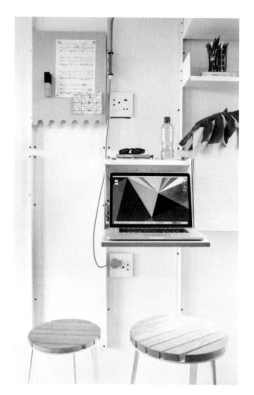

And the white-painted walls, cupboards and shelves make the small room appear bigger than it actually is. The atmosphere is far from cold or sterile, however, because the wooden elements, such as the floorboards, the folding table and various plywood boxes, introduce warmth to the room. The couple have managed to set colourful accents with the use of cheerful orange, blue and turquoise items, dotted around their home. For multiple purposes, a shelving system has been fixed to the walls, the elements of which can be changed as required. Instead of closed fronts, the homeowners opted for open shelving. It looks nice and light and sets colour accents. Several boxes provide flexible storage space. Khanyi and Dawn are not however in dire need of space – before they moved into their new tiny home, they cleared out a lot of unnecessary clutter. They found the experience of getting by with fewer things liberating. It gives them a wonderful feeling of freedom. ∎

Desk 'lite': a socket, a small shelf and space for the laptop – that's all one needs.

Sideboard, kitchen table or a very large board: the table can be unfolded or refolded, as required.

View of the desk from the kitchen table. The floor-to-ceiling window gives a view and an impression of spaciousness.

Sleeping under a starry sky:
no wonder the bed is
everyone's favourite place.

The tiny bathroom comprises only a toilet, sink, shelf and mirror.

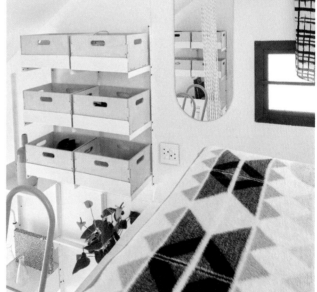

The steep roof makes for generous room height. There is even space for a tall mirror.

Design element, fresh air supply, view: the porthole is indispensable.

INSIDE & OUTSIDE Folding metal tables are generally used in the garden. But why exactly? They also look great in the living room and in the kitchen. Smaller tables, such as these Flips from richard-lampert.de, serve as putting-down tables in the hallway or the bathroom.

A pretty practical pair

Everything
IS FOLDABLE

Folding furniture doesn't just work when camping. Veritable space miracle, they are great to live with all year round.

CO-WORKER Fold it away, end of working day. hartodesign.fr have made Gaston to take care of and store all office equipment stylishly in drawers and compartments. When the work is done, the desk is simply folded away.

Who hasn't experienced this: all your friends have come to the birthday party and it's getting pretty tight around the dining table. No problem if you can quickly get some folding chairs and tables from the loft – furniture that is just perfect for such emergencies. Folded, they can be stowed away to save space and won't get into the way. And because they are so light and easy to carry around, they can also be used outdoors. Folding chairs and tables spend most of their existence in a corner, however.

Anyone who lives in a tiny home should rethink – foldable furniture is an excellent solution for small spaces at any time. If you have to perform different tasks in a single room, you can hardly afford to ignore these clever devices. In the evening the bed is folded down; in the morning it turns into a sofa once more or disappears into the cabinet. A table that can be folded down from the wall turns into a home office or becomes the focus of an intimate dinner party. ∎

AMBIVALENZ

Malte Grieb likes it plain, but with a certain something. It's logical that his Ambivalenz brand should bear the label 'inconspicuous'.

Anything there?

When the Ambivalenz furniture pieces are folded up and hang on the wall, you might look right past them, they're so flat and unobtrusive. No wonder, the linear design ensures that the furniture measures only a few fingers thick. Whether chair or wall shelf, cloakroom or table – only once they are unfolded to reveal their full glory do they become noticeable. If you opt for a colourful design it's all very different, however, for now the folding furniture turns into a cool 'optical wall object'.

HOCUS-POCUS
By sleight of hand, the home office consisting of a chair, shelves and desktop is magicked away.

A place to dream away

ONE FOR ALL Curt comes by himself, but he combines well with similar modules to create large seating and lounge areas. So a footstool pouffe becomes an armchair, sofa, lounger – thanks to a clever connecting system.

ALL-ROUNDER
A shelf wall such as this one from stringfurniture.com serves many different purposes. Books can be lined up here as well as clothes or dishes. A folding table complements the universally useful furniture item.

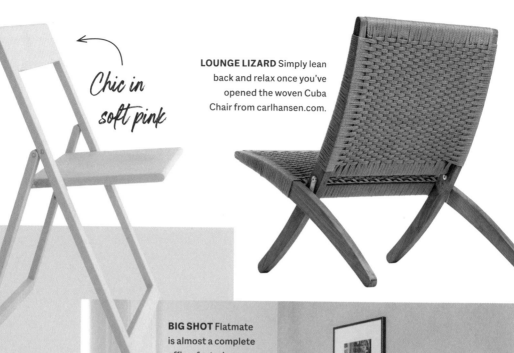

Chic in soft pink

LOUNGE LIZARD Simply lean back and relax once you've opened the woven Cuba Chair from carlhansen.com.

PURE & SIMPLE Aviva from magisdesign.com folds down its seat wherever anyone would like to use it. Those who prefer things more comfortable choose the model with armrests.

BIG SHOT Flatmate is almost a complete office, featuring lights, pen and note holders and storage space in the base structure. After work, nothing shows but an inconspicuous unit on the wall (muellermoebel.de).

3 COOL TIPS

Clack and gone. Unfortunately, not everything in an apartment is as flexible as **FOLDING FURNITURE**. But the most important things are ...

Table

Tables are needed for innumerable purposes, be it to eat at or just to put down a glass, to work at, to prep food, to craft or to play. The models are just as diverse as the different functions they fulfil. Small side tables can be hidden behind a sofa to save space. Kitchen, work and dining tables can be mounted on the wall and folded open when needed. Free-standing tables can also disappear quickly when they're in the way. Desktops and bedside tables are available as wall models or free-standing and foldable.

Chair

You can never have enough seating – for family and friends, in the kitchen and around the dining table, in the living room and on the balcony, at the desk and in the children's room. There is a foldable piece of furniture for every occasion – and it makes space for other pieces when it is not needed. Use folding chairs made of wood, aluminium or plastic whenever you want to sit upright. If you'd like to be more comfortable, foldable lounge chairs are a better choice. Even settees can be assembled from modules and stowed away again.

Bed

If you think of a folding bed, a narrow camp bed comes to mind. Wrong! There are so many comfortable and pretty pieces of furniture on which you can comfortably sleep at night and which look entirely different during the day. A daybed, for example, is a bed in the evening and a sofa in the morning. This transformation is even more pronounced for a sofa bed, available in a wide variety of widths and lengths. Blankets and pillows can be stowed in baskets or boxes during the day. And in a foldaway bed, the bed and the duvet are simply folded up.

Michael's racing bike needs to stand in the living room, but here it makes for an original furnishing.

New in
NEW YORK

Michael and Iris moved from the relaxed city of San Francisco to the vibrant West Village in Manhattan, swapping a spacious house for a miniature retreat.

The creative couple adore the animated life on their doorstep. They gladly accept the reduced space of a tiny apartment to live in this neighbourhood.

"The trick?
Don't clutter
the rooms!

The Bertoia Diamond
Armchair is
comfortable and looks
fabulously light.

Storage
space in every
corner – there
is room for
this and that
even above
and inside the
benches.

Michael and Iris are truly cosmopolitan. The Dutch stylist and the American creative director met in Düsseldorf in Germany, lived there for a few years and then moved to San Francisco. The couple are fans of the mid-century style, and they lived in a 1950s bungalow designed by Joseph Eichler. Recently, they packed their bags to start new jobs in New York. They love West Village and enjoy the shops, bars, cafés and theatres in their new neighbourhood. In return, they are more than happy to accept the minor disadvantages. They swapped their spacious house on the West Coast for a modest 33 sq m (355 sq ft) in the Big Apple. Preparing for the move included taking a close look at all their possessions: what was really important and frequently used? And what could they happily do without? Much of their surplus was sold, given away or put into storage - only the

Even with their
third roommate,
Miles, the corgi,
things won't be too
tight for them in
this apartment.

When the sliding doors
are open, both rooms
look like one. The
continuous floorboards
enhance this effect.

bare essentials made their way to the New York apartment. In their new, much smaller home, even the smallest corner is used as valuable storage space. There is useful additional room under the bed and inside the kitchen benches, for example. The walls and the built-in furniture are painted a light cream colour to give the apartment a feeling of brightness and airiness. Thanks to their metal legs, the sofa, armchair and bed also exude a certain lightness and almost seem to float. The greatest highlight, however, is the sliding doors between bedroom and living room – they are covered with large mirrors and, when closed, give the rooms an extra dimension. It's a wonderful way to live in the Big Apple. ∎

Everything is made to measure: the petite bed just fits between the two built-in wardrobes.

The tiny bathroom is attractive and bright. Flannels and other accessories provide splashes of colour. As elsewhere in the apartment, the original floorboards were retained.

In the kitchen and throughout the apartment the built-in cupboards reach up to the ceiling, creating space for all needs.

Smart
KITCHENS

A kitchen is much more than the
room in which meals are prepared,
so it deserves your full attention.

From breakfast to midnight snack,
from important discussions to stand-
up parties – there's always something
going on in the kitchen. The focus of
family life and the heart of the home,
it is where all the threads come
together. In a tiny home, the kitchen
space is naturally limited, but if it does
all you need it to do and the feel-good
factor is right, the total surface area is
of little importance.

In a small kitchen you have to
limit yourself to the bare necessities.
Of course, your favourite cookware,
utensils and gadgets should find their
proper place, but if you reduce your
household to the essentials, you can
make better use of the valuable space
in the cabinets and on the surfaces.

If the house structure permits it,
it's a good idea to open the kitchen up
to the living room. A wall may have
to be torn down to make this possible,
but it is worth the effort and the
temporary inconvenience because
it will turn a cramped space into a
friendly open-plan kitchen-diner-living
room. A kitchen island with storage
space underneath and seating visually
separates the cooking area from the
rest of the room. Alternatively, a large
dining table can create a link between
the kitchen area and the living room. ■

AT YOUR SERVICE Flexibility
is particularly important in
small rooms. A simple kitchen
trolley like the one below from
housedoctor.com serves as
a work and storage surface,
and it can be pushed aside at
any time if it's in the way.

BLACK & WHITE Black makes small rooms narrow and dark? Not if it's just the colour of the cupboards whereas the walls are a bright and shiny white. Dark wall units can be overwhelming, so open shelves could be a better choice.

Nice and flexible: spot on!

SHOW ME Quite a lot can be hidden behind closed cupboard fronts, so that the room looks tidy and appears larger. But sometimes an open solution may be more practical, such as this shelf on wheels from housedoctor.com.

STADTNOMADEN

Designers Linda and **Oliver Krapf** founded Stadtnomaden (or Urban Nomads), their brand for flexible urban living, in 2006.

Rolling Stone

The underlying idea for the company is that urban nomads yearn for a feeling of freedom and independence. They want to gather up their tents and travel light, but at the same time they also want to put down roots and long for stability. This is exactly where the Stadtnomaden furniture brand comes into play.

Their multiple award-winning products are characterized by stylishness, lightness and flexibility. Whether bed or room divider, every item is a multi-tasker. Plus everything is made sustainably, for a long, nomadic life.

À LA CARTE are the kitchen modules by stadtnomaden.com. Any number of individual modules can be selected, combined and arranged as required.

REINTERPRETED The good old kitchen buffet has been relaunched. The SieMatic 29 solitaire not only conceals a lot of space for pots and dishes, the multifunctional kitchen furniture also comes with a sink and hob (from siematic.com).

CHANGE OF DIRECTION If there is no space next to the sink to let the dishes drip dry, then they can simply dry above the sink. Basically a good idea to create more valuable work space.

Goes with the metal frame

WOOD-METAL-STONE This free standing module from framacph.com appears more like a piece of furniture than a kitchen unit. And yet it delivers everything you could wish for in a tiny kitchen.

3 COOL TIPS

It doesn't have to be large – as long as it's well planned. These ideas will make your **KITCHEN** appear much more spacious.

Storage

Pots and plates, toasters and thermos flasks, teaspoons and tomato soup – countless utensils and foodstuffs have to be stored. That's why storage space is an essential requirement in a kitchen. If lack of space stops you extending your kitchen cupboards sideways, just go up in height. Tall cabinets that reach up to the ceiling provide a surprising amount of space. A 45cm (18in) wide dishwasher is sufficient? Perfect, as this will leave more space for storage. Incidentally, pull-out cabinets give easier access than those with doors.

Surface

Cutting and peeling, boiling and kneading, stirring and grating – work happens every day in a kitchen and so plenty of working space is required. A rule of thumb is that you should allow 50 cm (20 in) of space for prepping. However, most amateur chefs will tell you that more really is more, so it's a good idea to banish as many kitchen appliances as possible into the cupboards and only take them out when you're using them. Pull-out worktops and mobile kitchen trolleys are another practical way of expanding the work area.

Look

Just because a room is small, it doesn't have to look small. Using a few tips and tricks, a kitchen can be made to look more spacious and open. Light plays a vital role. Windows, recessed lights, lamps – they all create brightness. And light is well reflected by high-gloss cupboard fronts. Another important point is the choice of colour: light, pastel-coloured walls make the room appear larger than it is. The cabinets can also be painted in light tones. And if you can do without handles, you'll gain calm, visually generous surfaces.

The white room-length cabinet hardly stands out visually, making the beautiful exhibits much more eye-catching.

" Simplicity is the greatest challenge

Michael, together with your colleagues you design entire buildings, interiors and even furniture. Do you aim for a typical look?

We try to avoid following a specific style or creating a signature company look. Instead, we prefer to individually cater to our customers' needs and to give each home its own personality. However, there's something that defines all of our projects –a great love of detail and a certain playfulness. Special accents, for example, can easily be set even in a predominantly white room.

What do you love about your job?

The people. I love meeting new people with each new project. I love the people we collaborate with. And I love the people on my team who are just great to work with. I also like challenges. The more difficult the project, the more complicated the implementation, the more likely we are to surpass ourselves in order to find the perfect solution. It is quite simply extremely satisfying to use our creative ideas and innovations to make our customers' lives more enjoyable and satisfying.

THE MAN FOR URBAN FLAIR

Michael K. Chen founded his architecture office MKCA, based in New York, in 2011. Yet he also transmits his in-depth knowledge of urban living as a lecturer and author.

What is the greatest challenge when it comes to furnishing small apartments?

We always try to integrate as many different functions as possible into the available space. In small rooms, in particular, many items have to be specially made and tailored to the space and the situation. And that's the crux of the matter: creating novel designs which combine all the necessary features and functions, yet still display a clean, unfussy look. And of course everything has to be user-friendly and be very easy to operate by the future residents. Simplicity is the key here.

And what do you love about designing and furnishing tiny homes?

I am convinced that smaller living spaces, that is, homes with a smaller footprint, are the solution to making life in the big cities more affordable for the residents, more sustainable in ecological terms and more vibrant. Every little space must be used sensibly, no detail is superfluous. In addition, such projects and ideas can also be transferred to other areas of communal living, such as student dormitories or shared residential facilities for the elderly, as well as apartments for families or individuals. ■

Apartment No 1

Ceramics are among Michael's favourite materials. The interior designer uses vases and sculptures to set accents and focal points.

The dining area merges seamlessly into the living area, which is inhabited by informal seating furniture. The highlight, however, is the pull-out television set that is hidden inside the closet.

Yet another well-used corner: this one offers space for a bar right next to the dining table.

Thanks to the custom-made furniture in the dining area, this space looks as if it has been cast from a single mould.

Calm, soft colours and clear
lines – it is easy to sleep
peacefully in this bedroom.

The kitchen cabinets don't reach right up to the ceiling, making the room look airier. The cupboards are deep, so there's plenty of storage space.

Apartment No 1

WHO? A working couple

WHERE? West Village, New York

WHY? Modernization and conversion

FAVOURITE FEATURE? The restrained but expressive materials used in the apartment's interior design

The niche in the wall next to the bathroom door is used as a shelf – a nice surprise.

The kitchen was moved from the margins to the centre of the apartment. The narrow galley opens on three sides.

A HUT INSIDE THE HOUSE
Here, the concept of a room within a room was taken even further. The separated-out area looks like a small log cabin, with a window and a log wall. The bedroom is on the upper level.

Up here to sleep, please!

Clever
ROOM SOLUTIONS

If large life is to take place in a small area, individual solutions must be found, for example creating a room within a room.

BOOKCASE To create more peace and quiet at the desk, the study is separated from the rest of the room by two floor-to-ceiling shelves. The wide passageway allows sufficient daylight to pass through.

Cooking, eating, sleeping, working, washing, playing, meeting, chilling – there's usually a lot going on in a home. All of these activities and more require space and 'accessories', that is, the right furniture and utensils. If the floor area is insufficient to give each activity its own space, it has to be rethought. What can you combine? How can you best maximize the available space? And where can you create additional space? Maybe the purposes of some of the rooms could be swapped over?

In order to rethink and plan completely anew, it is a good idea to turn the floorplan upside down. Does every room really have to be used as it currently is? Or could assigning it a different function perhaps create a better quality of life? There is a clever solution for every challenge. It's often a good idea to integrate new rooms into existing ones. The easiest way to envisage the outcome is to use wall paints or floor coverings that identify and delineate the individual areas. If the floor space is large enough, the new room can then be separated off by partition walls or shelves. If the ceiling is high enough, a new room can also be created at a high level, extending the space vertically. ■

SPACE FOR ALL THE STUFF

Divided rooms are, of course, smaller still. To create a feeling of space, built-in furniture is a good solution, because an ensemble of different shelves and chests of drawers 'clutter' the room visually. This room even has space for a cosy reading niche.

Board + brackets = table

VERSATILE The New Order cupboard from hay.dk offers open or closed storage space, exactly as needed. And when it is stacked, the unit morphs into a flexible room divider.

UNDER ONE ROOF

The bedroom is open to the bathroom – a bit like in some hotels. Without wall or door, the light is able to flood both rooms, making them seem lighter and more spacious. The toilet is hidden in an alcove for privacy.

BUNK BED The sleeping level is perched above the small living room like a bird's nest. Delicate curtains make the bunk nice and cosy.

BEZMIRNO

Yaroslav Pavlivskyi and **Andriy Gusak** are architects. Their Bezmirno studio is based in Kyiv, where they design houses as well as interior furnishings.

True to principles

Bezmirno in Ukrainian means something like immeasurable, infinite, and indeed the ideas of the two architects when planning the interiors of small apartments know no limits. However, they always stay true to their convictions. Nobody likes tight spaces, so the maxim: 'the more free space, the better' applies. And even if the space is limited, storage space is vital. The architects stayed true to these principles in the project on the left. With its inconspicuous storage space, the apartment appears spacious and light despite measuring only 40 sq m (431 sq ft).

HERE AND THERE In this Bezmirno home, the kitchen counter separates the living area from the kitchen. It also provides storage space.

HIGH-FLYING Seemingly floating chests of drawers can be stacked all the way up to the ceiling, providing plenty of storage space. Yet they appear more delicate than standing cupboards.

LIVING CUBE The cube's free-floating steps lead up from the kitchen to the lounge level. A railing delimits this area.

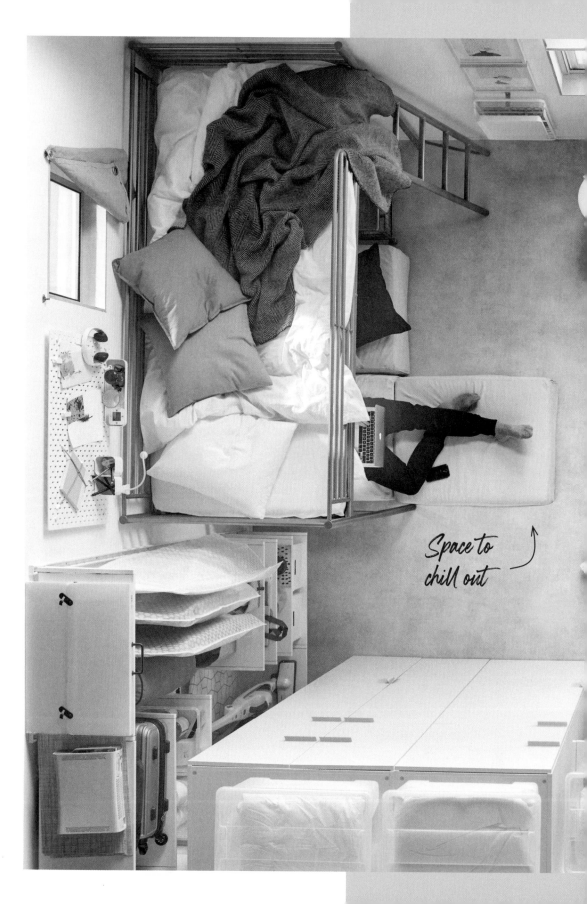

Space to chill out

ON THE MOVE Those who don't
want to commit to built-in
components can set up a loft bed
on the second level – and place the
sofa underneath. All the other
furniture pieces in this one-room
apartment are of course also
beautifully light and flexible.

INTO THE CORNER

Shelves and clothes rails transform the potential problem area of a sloping roof into a spacious wardrobe. The niche beside it houses a small stylish bathroom.

ALL TOGETHER

From night-time reading to bed linen, from woolly socks to cuddly pillows – there is space for all of life's necessities in this bed's generous storage space. It has room not only at the foot end, but also above the head and under the mattress.

3 COOL TIPS

If you have more life than space,
you need a **ROOM WITHIN A ROOM**.
This can be set up in different ways

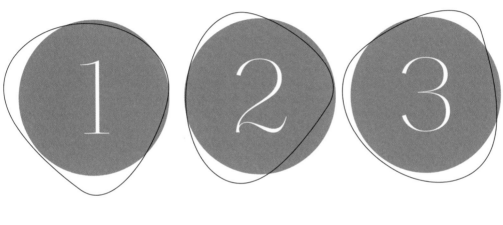

separate it

Whether you use a lightweight wall or a shelf, a cupboard or a screen, a partition can turn a small section of a room into a very personal space. It's perfect, for example, for the home office in the bedroom – a tall bookshelf or a screen will hide the desk so you cannot see the unfinished work from your bed. And if the children's room is large enough, a lightweight partition with a sliding door can divide the room into two. It's always important, however, that both of the two newly created rooms receive sufficient daylight.

raise it

Sometimes the area is not large enough to allow for a vertical separation. In that case, a horizontal division may work. A platform creates different areas that are only separated from each other by a few steps. The rooms do not appear to be completely separate from each other, but they are two independent areas. The advantage: an infinite amount of storage space can be integrated underneath the platform. You can store all sorts of things in drawers and boxes, even the bed, for example, which you can pull out in the evening.

lift it

Old buildings in particular often benefit from amazing room heights. These are perfect for adding a second level to the room. A loft bed is the most common addition. You sleep upstairs, and underneath there is space for a desk, a couch or cupboards and shelves. Instead of a bed on stilts, you might also have the option of installing a cube inside your room. This creates a closed space on the lower 'floor'. However, it's important to plan so that enough daylight falls into the additional room.

Thanks to the high ceiling, the small floor area seems so much more spacious.

Up close to
NATURE

Linda lives with her family where others mainly grow fruit and vegetables – in an allotment garden at the Copenhagen city gates.

Linda, Mads Mathias and little Gullmai enjoy the holiday feeling in their close-to-nature home away from the big city.

The daylight that
enters via the skylights
considerably reduces
the electricity bills.

Handleless doors merge with the wooden panelling. This door opens to reveal a refrigerator.

Two small lofts serve as play and guest rooms. Vertical struts ensure safety.

Linda was still in the middle of her architectural studies when she and her husband Mads Mathias visited a friend who lived in an allotment colony outside Copenhagen. The couple spent a lovely afternoon with their friend – and discovered a plot of land that was waiting for new owners. They fell head over heels in love with these 260 sq m (2,800 sq ft) of land and with the entire neighbourhood where numerous small, brightly painted houses, most of them built by their owners, peered out from among the redcurrant bushes and apple trees. A little hesitant at first, but encouraged by her husband, Linda set out to design their house. It had to be small, yet provide sufficient space for two adults, two children and the occasional guest. It was to fit harmoniously in between the apple trees, but still make a statement. And the couple also wanted it to be functional and sustainable.

The resulting home fulfilled all their needs and wishes – and also looked really attractive. In the midst of old trees and bushes, there now stands a small building with 80 sq m (860 sq ft) of living space, sufficient for the

The built-in shelves and the desk are made from the same wood, so everything looks harmonious and well matched.

Mads Mathias is a singer and musician. His music room is housed in the extension.

family to live and work. The kitchen, which is open to the roof, forms the focal point and heart of the house. On either side of the kitchen is a cube, each hiding a room inside as well as a play area and guest accommodation on top. Mads Mathias is a musician, and he now has a music room in a cube-shaped extension. Clad with wood from the ground to the roof ridge, the house also has interior walls and ceilings constructed from spruce wood – a 'must' for Linda, who is a Swedish national and for whom a house made with any other building material than wood is simply unimaginable. To prevent the wooden planks from darkening over time, they were given a special UV-resistant varnish. The wood and the deep windows allow nature into the house. Plenty of daylight also enters the rooms thanks to the large windowpanes and a number of skylights. This is not only functional, it also saves electricity. In summer, life takes place mainly on the terrace and in the garden. No wonder, for after all it was the green outdoor oasis that the couple initially fell in love with. ■

The skylight above
the settee introduces
additional daylight
into the room.

The narrow corridor to the bedroom looks more spacious thanks to the mirrored doors of the built-in wardrobe. Light enters through the narrow window under the roof.

The white walls create a calming, cool atmosphere in the bedroom.

" *I love that the light makes everything look so spacious*

There is only enough room for a shower, so the children bathe in an old tin tub.

In summer, life largely takes place outdoors. The fruit trees dictated the exact position of the house on the land.

METALLIC Off into your basket, you scarves and gloves, you hats and shawls, you blankets and bags! The wire baskets from korbo.se house simply everything. If you like it even tidier, the baskets are lined with a non-transparent fabric that hides any mess.

Also in copper and brass

Neat & tidy
HALLWAY

Narrow, dark and neglected: the hallway is often the forgotten stepchild in a home. However, that can easily be changed.

AGAINST BOREDOM
A hook bar is extremely useful, but colourful hooks, arranged where and how you like, are more attractuve. These ones are from bungalow.dk.

You don't get a second chance after a first impression, and this is why the often neglected hallway deserves a lot of attention. After all, this is the home's calling card – the hallway is the first thing visitors see when you open the door to them. You are also constantly crossing this area, on the way from the bathroom to the living room, to the kitchen and the bedroom. Who'd want to walk through a messy hallway and stumble over bicycle helmets, backpacks and countless pairs of shoes?

Two aspects make this functional room an inviting one: the first is its homeliness. Of course, a hallway should do its job. It offers storage space for a variety of things – from bunches of keys to umbrellas and skateboards. It is here that you take off your dirty Wellington boots and put down your wet umbrellas to dry.

Yet despite these utilitarian aspects, a hallway should also be inviting and create a positive atmosphere. The second important aspect is orderliness. If all the objects have their regular places, if everything is tidily stowed away, a narrow hallway is quickly transformed into a bright and friendly place that greets guests and always welcomes you home. ■

DELICATE Graceful but also pretty sturdy – shelving from moebe.dk can be assembled to your personal taste and fits into the smallest of corners.

CAR MÖBEL

Tim Küstermann runs the family business in the second generation – his father founded Car Möbel more than 50 years ago.

A good mix

The love for beautiful yet pragmatic living has evidently been passed on to the next generation in this company. What began in the 1960s as a retailer for DIY furniture has developed into an online shop for Scandinavian design.

Furniture and accessories, tableware and textiles from numerous manufacturers can be found here, as well as exclusive own-brand objects. There is also a range of perfect items for living in a limited space and for hallways – space-saving, flexible and well thought-out, with a timeless design.

BEHIND THE SCENES Jackets and coats, bags and shoes are well hidden behind the Push mirror from skagerak.dk. Perfectly tidy.

Made of solid oak

VERSATILE A horizontal plank forms the center of the Zutik wall system from alki.fr. Coat hooks and ladder shelves, shelves, mirrors and even sound-absorbing panels turn the whole wall into a piece of furniture. Perfect for all those who like to surround themselves with personalised solutions.

TAYLOR-MADE Instead of ready-made solutions, a very individual plan is usually the best choice. A wall coat rack, a few hooks and a sideboard with seat cushions are here united in a small space. The highlight is the idiosyncratic wallpaper which unites all individual parts as a harmonious ensemble.

MULTIPLE Hanging on a hook and creating space for eight more – the hanging wardrobe from sidebyside-design.de.

Stylish hanger

FULL OF CHARACTER A hanger might as well look impressive, after all, it is not constantly covered by jackets and coats. This one is from estampille52.fr.

ONCE UPON A TIME This shabby chic coatrack from iblaursen.dk is a reminder of the good old days. Freestanding, it can be used from both sides and wonderfully double as a room divider.

ROLLABLE Storing a vast amount in a very tiny space – this compact wardrobe from car-moebel.de offers a clothes rail as well as compartments for shoes, scarves and other essentials. And with its open back wall, it can also double as a room divider.

SPORTY The design of this neat, industrial look cloakroom bench called Goran is reminiscent of the changing rooms in old gyms.

NO BARS It doesn't always have to be a clothes rail. Pretty hooks are often sufficient. This combination of storage space and mirror is very practical (impressionen.de).

TWICE AS NICE A place to sit down in the hallway is extremely helpful. This old bench not only adds charm to the room, it also serves as a shelf to put down shopping bags and the like. The two wicker bags, which hold everything that shouldn't be lying around, are just as practical.

3 COOL TIPS

Stowing away, dressing and undressing,
getting from A to B – there's a lot going on in
a **HALLWAY**. Be prepared for these activities.

Stowing away

It's not ot only jackets, coats and shoes that need to be accommodated in the entrance area. Wellington boots and sports equipment, umbrellas and bicycle helmets are also stored here. Storage space is a must, but massive cupboards make a small hallway appear even more cramped. It is better to choose delicate furniture that doesn't overwhelm with its presence. If there is hardly any room for storage, these considerations are worthwhile: Can you store some things in the basement or in the loft? Can summer and winter jackets be changed over seasonally?

Dressing

Shoes on and shoes off, jacket on and jacket off, hat on and hat off – a lot of dressing and undressing happens right behind the front door. It is best to take a seat while lacing up your shoes, even if you only sit on a folding stool that is stashed away behind the cloakroom after use. Even more practical and convenient, of course, is a small bench which in addition conceals valuable storage space under its seat. A low cupboard, however, with a few cushions, can also be used as a seat and works just as well.

Looking

Do hat and hair look right and does the scarf go with the jacket? For many people, a look into the mirror is a must before they are going out. So it's simply essential in the hallway. No problem, mirrors can be hung on the wall to save space. Large mirrors not only reflect you from head to toe, they also make the hallway appear larger. Of course, the same applies to long mirrors that are integrated into clothes racks. Good lighting is important. And by the way, several lights have the added benefit of making athe hallway appear larger.

" *I enjoy freely experimenting with the available space*

Where partition walls once unfavourably divided the room, there is now light and airiness.

YOU JUST HAVE TO THINK OUTSIDE THE BOX

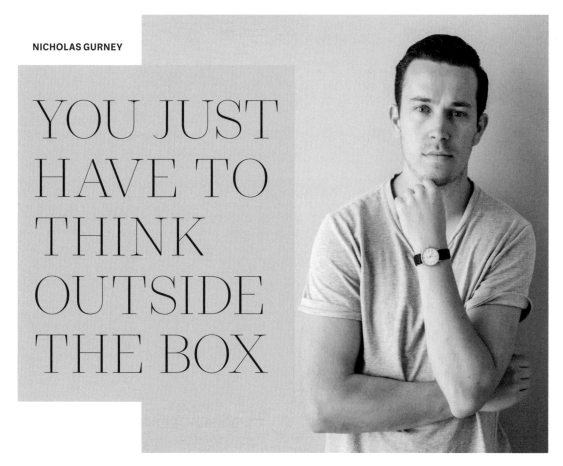

Australian **Nicholas Gurney** swears by minimalism, and tiny homes are his hobby horse.

Nicholas, you design cool living spaces with your company. How did you get there?

I'm actually an industrial designer, but I've always been interested in interior design and architecture. I couldn't find the right job and so I simply started my own business in 2011.

Living in small spaces is your speciality. Who are your clients?

The majority of my customers are young people, and often they are looking for their first home. I always make sure that the customer and I are on the same wavelength when it comes to lifestyle. This is how you get the best results.

Some of your designs are very bright and colourful. Which colours and materials do you like to work with best?

I like the entire colour palette. White has the greatest dynamism – although it is not actually a colour at all. In terms of the materials, I tend to choose low-priced ones which are easily available and – importantly – sustainable.

Your speciality is making the most of small spaces. What is the challenge there?

The obstacle that has to be overcome at the very beginning is people's fixed ideas. Who says that a room needs to be used only in one particular way? There are entirely new concepts for all those with little space helping them make the best possible use of a room.

What are the main advantages for those who consciously choose to live in a small home?

It feels really good to reduce your life to what is important. Living without an abundance of things or excessive furnishings gives you a feeling of contentedness. You can only feel this once you have thrown out the clutter. Plus a tiny home is, of course, also considerably less costly and less labour-intensive to run. ∎

The concept is to have lots of small spaces inside one large space. Sliding doors separate the areas.

Apartment No 1

WHAT? A one-room apartment

SIZE? 27 sq m (290 sq ft)

ASSIGNMENT? Preserving the view while creating light, air and living space

BEST FEATURE? The well-camouflaged black kitchen

This small living area differs significantly from those behind the adjacent doors.

The colours are reminiscent of Mighty Mouse, the cartoon character – they make the space look smaller than it is.

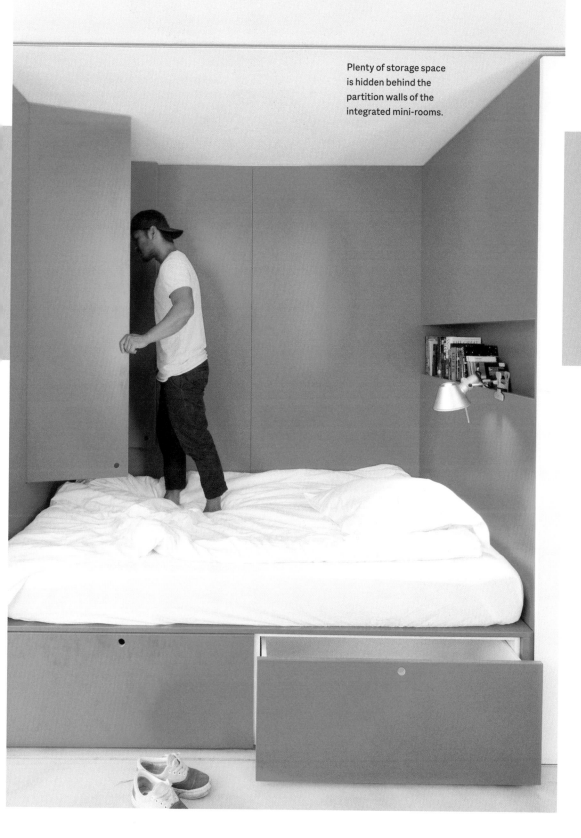

Plenty of storage space is hidden behind the partition walls of the integrated mini-rooms.

Both inside and outside walls are made from local pine which is not only cheap, but also sustainable.

In addition to the refrigerator and oven, there is even space for a washing machine.

Apartment No 2

WHAT? Accommodation for the family's guests and for short-term lodgings

WHERE? Sydney

SIZE? 20 sq m (215 sq ft)

BEST FEATURE? The extremely compact kitchen

The guesthouse was quickly assembled with prefabricated parts.

There is storage space under the bench seat as well as above it.

Everything is white and so the green wall units make for an exciting splash of colour.

Apartment No 3

WHAT? A one-room apartment with bathroom

WHERE? Sydney

SIZE? 22 sq m (237 sq ft)

BEST FEATURE? The raised kitchen with its inbuilt features and under-floor storage space

There is room under the kitchen platform for the mattress and countless other things.

The bed only comes out in the evening. It glides across the floor as if it were on a sledge.

The trick for creating space in this one-room apartment was to raise the floors, creating space beneath, which was possible thanks to the high ceiling.

ABOVE IT ALL There is usually plenty of space for hanging shelves above a desk. In this case, a niche was used to best effect, to accommodate both storage and the work surface. The white boxes hold all the odds and ends.

A glass top looks light

Valuable
STORAGE SPACE

From A for address book to Z for ziplock bag – every home is full of 'stuff'. How can you accommodate it all?

BEDDED DOWN The Marylin upholstered bed from schlaraffia.de ensures restful nights, and it can also be opened up easily to reveal plenty of storage space under the slatted frame.

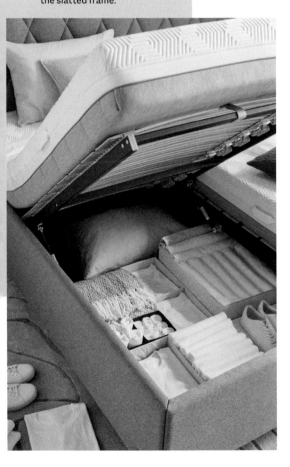

You don't have to be a hunter-gatherer to accumulate things in your home. It happens all by itself. Some people are strict and give away an old piece for each new one. Others find it hard to let go of things. The challenge is to accommodate all the accumulated treasures. Of course this applies to every home, but even more so to a small one. Firstly, there is less space. And secondly, order is particularly important in a tiny home, because the tidier it is, the more spacious and airy it will feel. Each object needs to have its own place. But where do you stash away all those lovely things? Before you start creating more storage space for your belongings, you should first take a hard look. Make an inventory and, if possible, rid yourself of some of the less important objects. It's a good feeling to sort out and declutter your home every now and then. You could, for example, tackle one drawer or a whole cupboard each day. If you have a little more time, you could just put all your things in the middle of the room and then separate the essentials from the unimportant 'stuff'. No matter how you proceed, only items that you really cannot do without are allowed to stay. Everything else is sold, given away or simply thrown out. ∎

TWO-TONE Put it on show or hide it? This sideboard from treku.com can do both. The attractive books are displayed, while all the necessary bits and bobs disappear behind closed fronts. The combination of lacquered and natural wood makes this gem of a furniture piece look friendly and warm.

FDB MØBLER

Diana Mot and **Isabella Bergstrøm** design together for FDB Møbler, a company that has exemplified Danish design for 80 years.

Please take a seat →

Highflyers

The two young women had barely finished their studies when their joint design Radius went into production at the traditional company. And the multifunctional furniture piece can do rather a lot: it's a table, bench and storage space, all in one. Like the other products in the series, Radius is particularly well suited for furnishing small houses and apartments.

BOXED IN Photo albums, records and a collection of board games – they all disappear inside a mini storage box. This one from moebe.dk is so pretty that it doesn't have to sit on a shelf, it can simply be displayed on its own.

SUCCESS STORY Originally, the architects from int2architecture.ru had planned this staircase for a specific apartment. However, it provides such valuable and stylish storage space that they now also delight other customers with it.

Slots of all shapes

The sideboard from
hubsch-interior.com
looks beautifully
light. It's made of
solid oak and offers
plenty of storage
space in its
compartments
for every part
of your home.

In two sizes

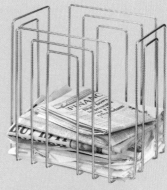

STACK 'EM HIGH Daily
newspaper and interior
design magazines have a
permanent place in the
Paper Collector, a classic
from the 80s. The design
looks nice and light, and
there's plenty of space
between the uprights.

MAKE ROOM This desktop
could of course have been
extended to both walls. But as
it is, it leaves enough room on one
side for a floor-to-ceiling shelving
unit, providing generous storage
space for files and the like.

ON TIPTOES The tall, narrow shelf from car-moebel.de not only provides enough space for all your favourite novels, it also has a closed drawer for reading glasses and other important items. And all that on a very tiny footprint.

CHEERFUL In the 3600 Container's five compartments you can stow away bathroom accessories, papers, toys and countless other small objects (magisdesign.com).

AS YOU LIKE IT Big or small, high or low – the cubes of the Eket system from ikea.com can be combined in any way that best suits a room and its occupants. Here a sideboard is complemented by a few cubes on the wall.

3 COOL TIPS

As the saying goes, there's room for all and room to spare. If you're looking for **STORAGE SPACE**, you may find it in the most unexpected places.

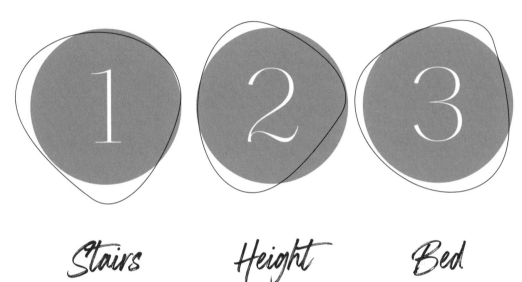

Stairs

Up and down. A staircase creates a link between different floors. Every now and then it also serves as a depositing place for things that are waiting to be taken up or down. Yet a staircase can do so much more – precious storage space is hidden beneath its steps. The simplest solution is to place fitted shelves or cupboards under the steps. More effective, however, is a carpenter-made solution that makes optimal use of the space below every single step. A curtain or a wooden panel makes the contents vanish from view.

Height

What's missing in terms of floor area has to be made up for by the height when you're living in a small home. Why should shelves and cupboards stop a few inches short of the ceiling? In the kitchen, for example, wall units that stretch right up to the ceiling provide significantly more space. What you don't often use is stored in the top compartments. In the bedroom, too, a wardrobe can reach all the way to the ceiling so that there is some space for what is rarely needed. And shelves for books or records provide additional space.

Bed

A bedroom should be neat and tidy – after all, this is where you want to relax. Storage space should therefore not be visible if possible. Luckily there is plenty of space under the bed. Some models have a bed box that is closed to the floor, providing space for everything that you want to disappear from view. If the mattress and slatted frame are raised on four legs, the space in between can be filled with shallow crates. Some manufacturers provide models with drawers and compartments under the slatted frame.

BIG LIFE
small space

'It may be only a small space but you can fit rather a lot of life into it.' That's how Rob describes his apartment in Cape Town, South Africa.

Rob loves Fifties-style furniture. No wonder that the armchair is one of his favourite places. The coffee table creates a cheeky splash of colour.

The gaze wanders unrestrained
from the balcony to the entrance
door, making the small room look
pretty spacious.

The kitchen unit merges
with a long storage unit.
The wooden fronts bring
warmth to the otherwise
cool room interior.

The storage unit's fold-down flaps make it easy to keep the room looking tidy.

The absence of handles on the cupboards under the stairs helps them to disappear into the background.

Rob, a film director in Cape Town, would have liked generous, wide spaces when he moved to the city. However, his small, dark apartment was entirely lacking in both of these. With a few clever tricks – and the support of an experienced architects' office – he transformed it into a cool, light-flooded home that not only has sufficient space for him, but also for sociable get-togethers with his friends. Trick No 1: light. A full-width window lets in plenty of sun and the open-room concept ensures that the light can flood the apartment unobstructed. Trick No 2: light colours. As hard as it was for Rob, the parquet flooring had to disappear under a thick layer of whited epoxy resin. The walls and cabinets were painted to match, for more light and air. Light-coloured wood makes the rooms feel warmer. Trick No 3: storage space. Different types of cupboards would interrupt the clear lines, which is why entire cupboard wall units run along the full length of the walls. One is half-height and transforms itself from a kitchen unit to storage for work and leisure items; the other one simultaneously serves as a staircase. Everything Rob needs is stashed away behind the plain, brightly varnished cupboard fronts. The result is 58 sq m (624 sq ft) of generous space, which gives Rob plenty of room for his busy and colourful life. ∎

With the help of
large sliding doors,
it was possible to
expand the living
area to include the
balcony, which also
provides lots of light
and magnificent
views of the sea.

White walls,
white floor – just
a few colour splashes
to punctuate
the clean look.

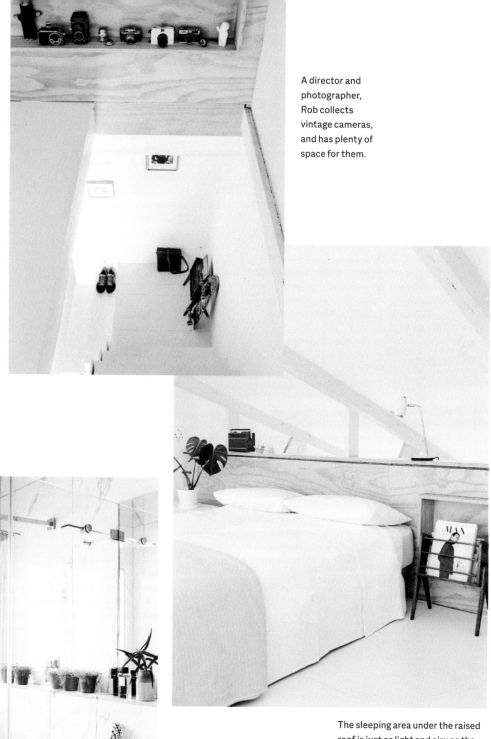

A director and
photographer,
Rob collects
vintage cameras,
and has plenty of
space for them.

The sleeping area under the raised
roof is just as light and airy as the
rest of the apartment.

Glass and marble-
look tiles transform
the narrow
bathroom into an
oasis of wellbeing.

One of many versions

REVERSIBLES When is a table not a table? With muellermoebel.de. Depending on how you place and turn it, the side table becomes a music stand or a shelf, a magazine rack or a stand for your notebook.

Flexible & PORTABLE

Sometimes here, sometimes there.
As life today is not static, it's convenient
to have furniture that can be moved.

BEST FOOT FORWARD
A trolley under the desk
is ideal for holding files,
magazines or a printer
and paper. It hardly takes
up any space and can be
moved around if need be.

Things change. While in the past
many people used to spend their lives
in just one place, today much of life is
in motion. People move from city to
city, and from one country to another.
Freedom and mobility – that's what
many of us strive for. The furniture
to match this lifestyle is light and
flexible. You can easily move it from
one place to another, and from one
room to the next. Even moving house
is easier with such furnishings. All
those who consciously choose to live
in small places, who do not wish to be
tied to one place and who keep their
belongings to a minimum, will find
perfect living solutions in portable,
flexible furniture.

Whether wardrobe or bed, of
course, mobile versions don't exist
for all items of furniture. Yet many
have the prerequisites that allow you
to lead the life of an urban nomad.
Shelves, for example, can be placed
on castors and pushed through the
entire apartment as needed. And
wheels will also turn sets of drawers
or serving trolleys into flexible objects.
Other pieces, meanwhile, can easily
be carried from one place to another
because they are light in weight. Some
side tables even come with handles
for this very purpose. ■

MOEBE

Martin de Neergaard Christensen, **Nicholas Oldroyd** and **Anders Thams** are united not only by their love of good design but also by their Moebe brand.

Good for everyone

The makers behind the Moebe brand attach great importance to sustainability, and they ensure their products are made in a fair and environmentally friendly manner. Their designs are consistently functional, plain and simply timeless, allowing people to enjoy their tables and shelves, lighting and home accessories for as long as possible. An item gets broken? No problem, you don't have to throw the beautiful piece away – the manufacturers have made sure that everything can easily be repaired so that you can enjoy it for the longest possible time.

HERE & THERE Does the coffee taste better outside? Simply carry your cups and the side table from moebe.dk onto the balcony.

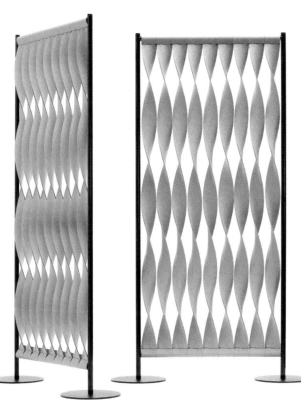

Ribbons of felt

SEMI-TRANSPARENT Make two out of one – the Flow room element from hey-sign.de separates one side of the room from another, without blocking the flow of light and air. Several elements can of course also be used together.

TOP DRAWER Open drawer, place stuff inside, close drawer. Drawers are superbly practical for storage. And on wheels, like here with Alex from ikea.com, they're always wherever they're needed.

WORK OF ART The TriAngle stool, composed of lots of triangles, looks like a sculpture rather than seating furniture (karakter-copenhagen.com).

VALET STAND Side table today, serving trolley tomorrow, assistant in the home office the day after – the House Doctor trolley makes for a very practical and elegant roommate.

ROLLING STOCK A shelf on wheels is everyone's best friend in tiny homes. It's always ready, offers plenty of storage space and can also be used as a room divider if so desired.

3 COOL TIPS

Not every piece of furniture is **FLEXIBLE** and **PORTABLE**, but with a grip or wheels you can transform some into itinerant assistants.

Sitting

How convenent that chairs are so easy to carry around, from the dining table to the terrace and back to the desk. Lightweight chairs with metal frames are particularly practical. And stools are even more flexible. Often they can be stacked in a corner until they are needed. For portability and convenience, bean bags and pouffes are also good choices. They can quickly be carried anywhere you want to make yourself comfortable. If they're in the way, just push them aside. Even armchairs and sofas are easily mobile if they are equipped with wheels.

Separating

Adding a partition is time-consuming and not always possible - or useful. A screen, however, will at least visually separate areas and is always ready to use. Looking at your desk makes it hard to fall asleep? A screen will block the view of the work area and of any unfinished work. And it just as easily separates the kitchen from the living area. Room dividers are exceptionally practical, especially in a tiny home, because they allow you to divide the home into different areas or to block out unwanted sights.

Putting down

If you're moving the seating furniture around, the spaces for putting things down also have to change place. Conveniently, many side tables are so light that they can easily be moved, and stools quickly transform into tables. In this way, you can quickly set up new favourite corners and create new rooms in a small area. But it's not only tables that are mobile - shelves, containers and serving trolleys, even entire kitchen islands, can be turned into flexible pieces of furniture with castor wheels, so they're quickly pushed aside.

Florian Kallus and **Sebastian Schneider** create their designs by constantly exchanging ideas with one another.

KASCHKASCH

EACH PIECE DOES LOTS MORE

Florian and Sebastian, you are trained carpenters, you studied product design and then you went on to found your product design studio kaschkasch in 2011. What kind of products do you design?

Our focus is on furnishings, from very large to very small. We design modular cabinet systems and sofa landscapes, for example, but we also create new furniture handles and wardrobe hooks, and vases as well as lamps. Our customers are both small and large-scale manufacturers of furniture, lights and home accessories.

What is distinctive abour your designs?

Our designs are primarily shaped by our collaboration. Discussion and discourse are extremely important to us. They help us to develop design ideas that challenge the conventional and the preconceived. Their beauty lies in their clarity.

What makes your job attractive and what are the main challenges?

We love the diversity and the freedom that different customers and assignments bring to us. The challenges are manifold from the design and the development to the creation of a successful product. It often takes one or two years until a new item is ready and approved for serial production.

You developed a furniture series especially suited to small rooms for the furniture manufacturer Müller. What are the best solutions for an acute lack of space?

The furniture needs to be multifunctional, but it shouldn't dominate the room. What we particularly like, among other things, is the fact that every detail has been carefully thought through. And this is particularly important for small rooms. ∎

A lot can be done with the limited space here

The Corner furniture series is designed for flexibility – whether table or cupboard, shelf or sofa, the items can all be cleverly combined.

Apartment No 1

FOR WHOM? Müller furniture workshops

WHAT? A modular furnishing system

WHERE? Everywhere there is little room

BEST FEATURE? The space-saving furniture pieces are multifunctional perfection

The sofa seats up to three people in the daytime and makes a comfortable bed at night. Pillows and blankets are stored in the hollow under the slatted frame until needed.

The cabinet offers cleverly divided storage space on the inside, yet it is unobtrusive on the outside.

The upholstered top turns this container into a practical seat.

Yvon has filled every room with vintage rattan furniture to add to the airy feel.

Loft-Style LIVING

High stucco ceilings and exposed brickwork,
open rooms and cool interiors – no, Yvon's apartment
is not located in the Big Apple, but in Amsterdam.

The artist loves her home in Amsterdam's lively De Pijp district. She shares it with Elvis and countless Buddha figures from her travels around the world.

A design
feature, this
light staircase
is hardly
noticeable.

The NY-style loft
extends over the
top two floors.

The kitchen cabinets are
plain and functional, the
creative decor individual.

How lucky that Yvon paused to think again before trying to sell her old apartment in Amsterdam's De Pijp district, because the artist actually loves this part of town, her friendly, creative neighbours and the vibrant life on her doorstep. But her small home was too cramped, too cluttered, too dark. Yvon yearned for more light and air. And after one or two flashes of inspiration and pauses for reflection, it became clear to her: she didn't need to move house to get this new ambience; she could achieve it simply by renovating. The work did, however, take nine months – and during this time the owner camped amidst building rubble, tarpaulins and machines. To create a genuine loft feeling, Yvon exposed the masonry on one wall. The light now flows unobstructed into the open space, and the new, free-floating wooden staircase does not get in the way. Instead of individual shelves and

cupboards, Yvon's belongings now live in a wall unit that stretches over the entire length of the upper floor. Two of the closet doors open to reveal a small bathroom. The cloakroom on the lower floor is similarly stashed away behind wooden panels. Another action she took was to put everything that was superfluous into storage. The only things that remained in her apartment were her works of art and the favourite pieces she discovered on her travels around the world. The furniture, which is mostly mid-century, is displayed to full effect in these bright, clean rooms. Instead of a narrow, dark space, the artist now lives in a New York-style airy and cool but cosy loft. ■

The vertical surfaces were finished with water-repellent paint, so there was no need for tiles.

Every nook and cranny provides storage space, making the sleeping area practical as well as cosy. Yvon sewed the new bedspread from towels.

No need to feel
claustrophobic:
the folding doors
allow air and light
into the miniature
bathroom. When
closed, they merge
with the wall unit.

Nicely sorted
CLOTHES

The elegant dress and the favourite blouse, the new shoes and the old leather jacket – they all need a place to live.

Of course, a large wardrobe always offers plenty of storage space, with its compartments, clothes rails and drawers. There is space for boxes and baskets on top. And stacks of T-shirts, jumpers, trousers and anything you don't want to see simply disappears behind its closed fronts.

Large wardrobes are not always the best choice, however, especially in small rooms. A flexible shelving system may be a more useful piece of furniture to choose. Or a few hooks plus compartments and mirrors, a clothes rail plus sideboard or a clothes rack and a chest of drawers – depending on the space you have to play with and your needs.

Personalized solutions allow you to make use of niches and to fill corners sensibly. Sloping ceilings become walk-in wardrobes. A self-assembled set provides plenty of storage space under the stairs. And the substitute wardrobe can even function as a room divider, separating the sleeping area from the home office area, for example, or acting as a seperator between the entrance hall and the living area. Another advantage is that, unlike the bulky body of a wardrobe, these alternative solutions will also bring lightness into your home. ■

HANG 'EM HIGH A simple rod suspended from the ceiling or screwed to the wall with spacers makes a perfect wardrobe, and soft baskets store everything that cannot be hung up. This one is from ikea.com.

CURTAINS UP Sloping ceilings and narrow niches are predestined to be transformed into dressing rooms. A well-planned shelving system featuring clothes rails and drawers houses the clothes, while a curtain hides the entire walk-in area.

Leather covers

EYE CATCHER The Imago hooks from materdesign.com are covered in leather and almost too pretty to be hidden by coats, scarves and bags.

ONE OF A KIND Here, the clever furniture from Frama gives a very personal touch to an entire wall surface.

NICE AND SIMPLE A plain metal frame acts as a clothes rail, perfectly setting the clothes in scene. And it's practical too as it takes up little space.

FRAMA

Niels Strøyer Christophersen does not like to be distracted by shapes and colours. It's his love for all things plain that is the focus of Frama.

Back to basics

Clear, simple lines and natural materials, soft natural tones and organic shapes: all products exude this pleasant calm, this naturalness. Whether Niels is designing candle holders or shelves, footstools or crockery – they are all devoid of any superfluous elements. Nothing unnecessary disturbs the eye. Honest and close to nature.

And because all his products are so beautifully simple and calm, they look particularly good in small apartments where they will discreetly stay in the background and adapt to every lifestyle without demanding attention.

WELL EQUIPPED It's just perfect when the manufacturer has thought of everything and offers a wide variety of features. This shelf front from stringfurniture.com has room for anything that hangs, disappears in drawers and lies in compartments. There are even shelves and hooks for sunglasses and umbrellas.

Individually configured

SIMPLE & FLEXIBLE It couldn't be easier – a wall cupboard hides trousers, shirts, jumpers and underwear behind its doors, while shoes can be placed underneath. A coat hook takes the hangers.

Must-have mirror

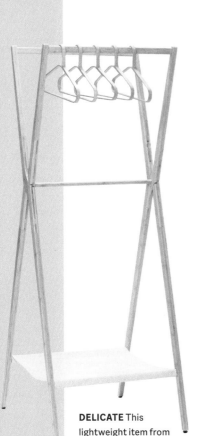

IN A LINE What used to be sold only in clothes stores has long since found its way into the bedroom: the clothes rack. Everything that is folded, meanwhile, can be accommodated in a cupboard on wheels.

DELICATE This lightweight item from hubsch-interior.com made of bamboo fits into almost any niche. The hangers take jackets, shirts and blouses, the cotton layer accommodates hats, scarves and bags.

HOMEMADE Of course, a simple coat rack is practical and can be used almost anywhere. If you'd like something a little more unusual, just grab a saw and drill. Draw a branch onto a plank of wood and then saw it out with a jigsaw. Buttons or hooks are easy to screw on. If you like, you can add a protective layer of varnish to your DIY coat rack.

Crafty DIY

Easy wrap around

ASSEMBLY LINE
Who says it always needs to be a shelving unit? A dresser offers room not only in its drawers but also has a top to put things down on. Plus, the clothes rail above holds everything free from creases.

BORDERLINE
Why should the wardrobe always stand against the wall? It works just as well as a room divider. An open shelving system appears airy and allows daylight to enter between the areas.

3 COOL TIPS

Some pieces hang, others lie down, and
some need to stand. There is a suitable space
for every item of **CLOTHING**.

Hanging

Anyone who configures
an open wardrobe system will
most likely integrate a clothes
rail. But where to put the
hangers if you're looking for
a personalized solution?
A clothes rack, for example,
is an excellent choice.
Some even have a few
compartments. Others are
particularly practical thanks
to their castor wheels.
Alternatively, a rail can be
attached to the ceiling, either in
a fixed or a flexible system. And
if you only have a few items of
clothing that need to be hung
up, you can simply use a few
pretty coat hooks.

Lying down

Jeans and T-shirts, jumpers
and sportswear, underwear
and nightwear: not all items
of clothing need to stored
on hangers. For many,
a compartment, a shelf
or a drawer are sufficient.
Of course, a shelving system
offers optimal storage space,
just as you like and according to
the space available. But if you're
looking for a partner for your
clothes rail, you could place
a chest of drawers or a cabinet
underneath. In addition to
a clothes rack, there is also
space for a narrow, tall shelf or
for wall cupboards mounted
one above the other.

Standing up

Whether in a cupboard or an
open system, you will also need
space for cartons, baskets and
boxes. After all, belts, scarves,
hats and gloves, for example,
all need to be accommodated.
Shoes, too, can be stored in
boxes. An open shelving system
definitely offers the right
space for this purpose.
Shelves specially designed
for shoes can also be added to
the system. If you assemble
your personal wardrobe,
you can store boxes and
baskets on top of or under
cupboards and chests of
drawers. Shoes are simply
lined up underneath.

All the utensils are hidden behind the cupboard doors. This way, the kitchen units look like one large, elegant piece of furniture.

A HOME
with a Soul

Interior designer
Nancy finds impersonal
apartments abhorrent.
For her, a home has to
reflect its residents.

During her time at
advertising agencies,
Nancy learned to work
within tight budgets.
That's why here she
combined vintage
furniture with some
new pieces.

Natural materials such as wood, leather, metal and soft fabrics create a warm atmosphere.

The loft inspired Nancy to use this cloud wallpaper, which perfectly matches the colour of the sofa as well.

Interior designer Nancy calls the art of turning an apartment into a home that reflects the soul of its residents the 'Flemish touch'. She knows what she's talking about – after all, she grew up in a Flemish family of architects. Professionally, however, she was initially drawn to Paris. There she worked first in the advertising industry, before going freelance as an interior stylist with an apprenticeship in room design. One of her projects was this small loft apartment, which she transformed into a domicile full of character. The 44 sq m (474 sq ft) urgently needed her professional input. The rooms had been unfavourably subdivided, the kitchen was tiny, while the entrance area was unnecessarily large. It took Nancy three months to transform the apartment into a cosy, contemporary home with plenty of personality. First of all, the walls were torn down and pipes and cables were relaid so that the area could be divided up more sensibly. The kitchen became the bedroom and the bathroom was transformed into the kitchen. The living room, meanwhile, extends into the former entrance hall. The small apartment

The window allows daylight to flood the hallway and at the same time visually enlarges the living area.

Nancy lives, eats and cooks
in one room, making the space
appear generous and open.

Modern colours, patterns and shapes make for a great bathroom.

immediately appeared much more spacious. Nancy also hides everything that is not pretty, and so the kitchen appliances had to disappear behind cabinet fronts, and tangled cables and electronic gadgets found their way into a wall unit. The radiator is also hidden behind the mesh of custom-made cladding. Storage space was urgently needed and has been made available across all rooms. In the bedroom, for example, shelves were fixed above the head of the bed, offering space for night reading. A built-in wardrobe extends across the entire wall opposite. The kitchen cabinets are all made to measure and offer plenty of storage space. While they and the bathroom cupboards are gleaming white, a soft petrol colour is used in the kitchen, living area and bedroom. Black and copper-coloured accessories provide accents. There is definitely no lack of personality in this apartment. ∎

Who would guess that this was once a narrow kitchen? The new bedroom is small, but bright and cosy.

Don't be afraid of dark colours: here they bring peace and comfort to the 'sleeping alcove'. The shelves are painted in the same colour and so are hardly noticeable.

On the WALL

If living space is limited, every square inch is precious, and it's best to switch to a third dimension.

Sofas and armchairs, tables and chairs – they will all happily stand freely in the room. This, however, is quickly filled up and the walls are then the only providers of storage space. Cabinets and sideboards have their place here – as long as the latter are not positioned across the room as room dividers. But the area is also limited in the vertical dimension; after all, space is already reduced by cupboards as well as by doors and windows. And of course you would also like to have space for pictures and other wall decorations.

Beware – if you now overload every remaining square inch with shelving, hanging cabinets and other such items, you'll quickly create a crowded feeling. Floor-to-ceiling shelves often take up a lot of space – but they're allowed to do so because they present a homogeneous surface and do not restrict the space. If you hang up a lot of smaller wall furniture and objects over a large area, however, you'll easily create a chaotic look. If you want to hang several small shelves, pinboards and pictures on a wall, it's best to arrange them in small groups. Not only does it look attractive, it also makes the wall look tidy and the room more spacious overall. ∎

STACKABLE It's as if someone had put a few crates on top of each other according to their whim – the wall modules from bloomingville.com look relaxed and casual. The cubes offer a lot of space for books and other beautiful things.

Elegant bulldog clips

LET'S HAVE A LOOK A pinboard can hold notes or become an exhibition space for postcards – Mesh from housedoctor.com can do both. And, additionally, it has a compartment for pens, notepads and notebooks. Clips of all kinds serve as fasteners.

HOOKED UP So simple, yet so clever – perforated metal rails run vertically up the wall and hold the shelves. The system fits every living space – this version is particularly elegant.

MARION

Marion Hellweg lives and works in Munich. Since 2010 she has been running her own creative design office with a focus on interiors and lifestyle.

Maxi solutions

A lively all-rounder, Marion Hellweg is very active as an author, journalist writing about design, lifestyle and architecture and the editor-in-chief of an interiors magazine. She also likes to lend a hand when it comes to making pieces.

A trained carpenter and interior designer, Marion has already designed the entire interior look of a large number of mini-apartments and small houses and then realized the designs together with her team. Her main focus is on 'big solutions for small spaces'. Since in a very small home every inch is precious, she pays particular attention to walls and wall niches when it comes to finding the best possible storage space for all the many pieces that need to be shut away.

AT A GLANCE Cooking utensils and other things hang on the kitchen wall within easy reach (iblaursen.dk).

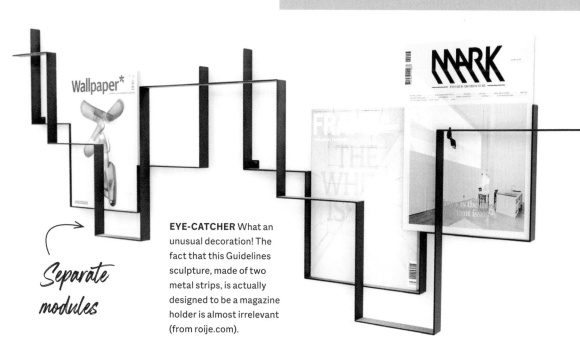

Separate modules

EYE-CATCHER What an unusual decoration! The fact that this Guidelines sculpture, made of two metal strips, is actually designed to be a magazine holder is almost irrelevant (from roije.com).

HEXAGON This honeycomb-shaped wall shelf from bloomingville.com can be subdivided into many small compartments, providing space for all your favourite things.

UP TO THE TOP A narrow desk like this one from the moebe.dk range of shelving systems does not take up much space, but instead uses the height of the wall. Shelves can be added as required.

IN THE SPOTLIGHT Instead of a wobbly pile next to the sofa, magazines are stylishly stored on the wall in the Norr magazine holder from skagerak.dk. The most beautiful publications can of course sit in the front row.

For magazines & pictures

REPURPOSED We know perforated panels mainly from workshops, but they can just as well be used in the living room, the home office or the children's room. Here, a number of elements are combined on one wall which is peppered with hooks, shelves and so on, as required (ikea.com).

PRETTY LITTLE THING One board, two brackets – that's all it takes to build a shelf? That may be true, but the design of this one from framacph.com is particularly successful.

In various colours

READY TO HAND
Nice, slim and pretty practical: the housedoctor.com magazine holder keeps reading matter close at hand by the sofa, ensures things are tidy on the desk and provides goodnight reading in the children's room.

STRUNG UP A clever idea: Magazine Hang Out holds your journals and magazines on strings. Thick wooden balls ensure they don't slip off (from bywirth.com).

3 COOL TIPS

If you have little space, simply hang furniture on the **WALL** instead of pictures. There are some clever and practical solutions.

Shelves

Shelving units provide storage space without appearing bulky and can grow in height when there is insufficient space on the floor. They can be used in a variety of ways, from a single shelf to a large bookcase. Shelves stand in front of a wall, but can also be hung up. Shelving systems that can be individually assembled are ideal for difficult situations. Ladder shelves and units that hang on rails look particularly delicate and are therefore perfect for tiny homes. Baskets and boxes hide small items to keep the open shelves tidy.

Pinboards

The classic pinboard holds shopping lists, notes and important reminders, postcards and photographs. But their modern relatives can do much more. Mesh walls or perforated panels not only hold notes, but can be made almost infinitely more useful with the right accessory. Hooks and brackets allow you to attach objects to the grids. A perforated wall is even more flexible. With the right accessories, it is not only useful in the workshop, but also around the house. You can even hang up shelves and containers.

Specials

Among the many resourceful ideas that make living in small spaces easier are tables that can be attached to the wall and opened down when needed. Whether as a desk or a dining table, this system works in many situations. Other clever ideas include racks for storing kitchen utensils. Hung up next to the stove, the frying pan and the whisk are always close at hand. Magazine holders that hang on the wall and keep your favourite magazines at the ready are also very practical. They are available in a wide variety of shapes and colours.

ADD A ROOM

PLUS ONE MORE ROOM, PLEASE

Erik Aarup is the CEO of the 'add a room' team. The Danish company has been selling cleverly devised modules since 2010.

A tiny private beach oasis. This module works just as well as an office or a guest room.

You have the best ideas when you think outside the box

'Add a room' - the name is the concept: you sell stand-alone modules which can also be combined to form a larger building.

Exactly. We construct different-sized rooms from wood. The cubes can be combined with one another, but they can also just as easily stand free on their own. It allows you to park a guestroom or an office room in your garden, or to position a holiday home on your favourite piece of land by the lake. The room modules are produced in different sizes and can be equipped with a large variety of different features. It depends entirely on the customer's needs and wishes.

And who came up with this idea?

The Danish founder, Susanne, developed the concept for 'add a room' together with her Swedish husband Sven. Susanne spent a long time working for Danish designers, while Sven gained plenty of experience working with wood as a material when he was a building contractor. In their company, the couple combine Danish design flair and Swedish know-how about building wooden houses.

Wood is a sustainable building material. Do you value sustainability in your work?

Absolutely. We work with natural materials and we build houses that are not static. They lend themselves to flexible uses, according to the needs of the owners. This also makes them more sustainable.

What are your favourite projects?

It's always a pleasure when the finished room module is put into place and blends perfectly with its surroundings. I'm always especially pleased when the original concept is shown to work as intended. This was the case, for example, when a Swedish family bought a holiday home and later added two more modules as the family grew. An additional study and office module now also allows them to extend their weekends.

What advice do you give to those who want to live in a small space?

Think carefully about which activities you can easily move outdoors. The living room is too small? A terrace of 20 sq m (215 sq ft) makes for a lovely space in summer. And if you build a generous outdoor kitchen, you'll only need a small kitchen corner inside the house. ∎

If there's no room inside the beach hut, the shower will simply go on the outside. The perfect place to rinse off sand and salty water.

Flexible living: sofa modules morph into a bed, while the side tables and a stool are always where you need them.

Apartment No 1

WHAT? A beach house for the TV programme House Doctor

SIZE? 20 sq m (215 sq ft)

WHERE? Hvide Sande, Denmark

BEST FEATURE? The view of the sea

The hotplate on the shelf makes for an improvised kitchenette. Utensils and ingredients are stored in baskets and boxes.

At the other end of the terrace a small sauna is hidden in a separate little house. It is heated with wood.

A miniature kitchen for quick meals. Cooking mostly happens outdoors.

Apartment No 2

WHAT? A former showroom for 'add a room'

SIZE? 15 sq m (161 sq ft) plus outdoor features

BEST FEATURE? The outdoor kitchen which links the sauna with the little houses

There is space for a living area as well as a tiny bathroom.

The wooden deck is spacious enough for summer outdoor living.

Sleeping
LIKE A DREAM

In a tiny home, the bedrooms are usually very small indeed. Yet that doesn't mean it has to feel cramped.

The smallest room in a home is often used as a bedroom. Basically that's a good idea, after all, you usually only spend a few waking hours there. That's no reason, however, to neglect this room and to waste no or only little thought on its design and furnishing. Using a few simple tricks, the narrow bed chamber can be transformed into a bright, airy and friendly room – for relaxed hours and sweet dreams.

The smaller the room, the more important it is to make the best possible use of the space you have. This is where custom-made products come into play. Solutions that are precisely tailored to the situation make optimal use of niches and corners. A made-to-measure bed under the sloping roof, for example, with a bed box that provides additional storage space for spare bedding and bed linen. Or a sliding door that turns the niche beside the chimney into a wardrobe.

It is important that none of the built-in components appear too massive and bulky in order not to overwhelm the small space. Correct lighting is just as important as making good use of space. Instead of gleaming ceiling spotlights, several small light sources create a cosy atmosphere. ■

WELL HIDDEN Box spring beds usually have a bed box with space for blankets and other bedding, but normal beds also have room under the slatted frame, which can be used for shallow crates or wide drawers.

Room for treasures

DOUBLING UP Well, it doesn't have to cover the entire wall. But large mirrors increase the size of a room not only visually, they also reflect the light, and a small bedroom will appear twice as airy and spacious.

FEATHERWEIGHTS Light shelf racks are a good solution for all small rooms. In the bedroom, they work well as a bedside table substitute next to the bed and for storage space above it (stringfurniture.com).

Also comes with sliding doors

Bed box as an accessory

SURPRISE, SURPRISE! The highlight of the Müller Nook bed is its headboard. Its top serves as a put-down place for books, glasses and handkerchiefs. But underneath, it boasts various hidden compartments for storing all sorts of things.

DESIGN ICON The stacking bed, designed by Rolf Heide in 1966, has long been a furniture classic. One bed becomes two in the twinkling of an eye.

MÜLLER

Jochen & Katja Müller run a long-established company. Müller has manufactured beds, tables and more for more than 150 years.

Small Living

What started as a very small outfit in 1869 has since developed into a large enterprise, working with well-known designers. Over the years, the company has become a specialist in furniture that takes up little room but is multifunctional.

Appropriately, the company's new name is Müller Small Living. Its special Corner line features clever, all-purpose designer furniture for micro-apartments, ranging from student accommodation to hotel rooms.

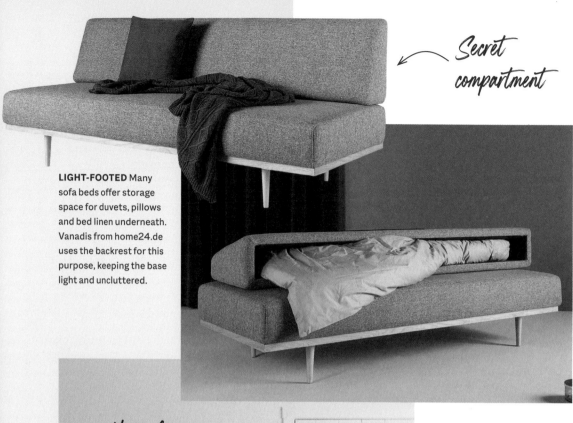

Secret compartment

LIGHT-FOOTED Many sofa beds offer storage space for duvets, pillows and bed linen underneath. Vanadis from home24.de uses the backrest for this purpose, keeping the base light and uncluttered.

Hung from leather straps

CLOSE TO NATURE
Shelf, cupboard, stool – no, thank you. A simple cylinder made of cork is used here. The table lamp with its delicate feet turns the ensemble into a pretty, unassuming bedside table with a natural touch.

INVISIBLE Flexible shelving systems with metal rails and planks are always a good idea. The brackets can be attached at different heights, meaning that you can sensibly use even the smallest niches and corners. In this system, everything is painted white like the wall, making the home-assembled shelf very unobtrusive.

SWEET DREAMS Plain bed linen appears calmer than patterned bedding, making it a better choice especially for small rooms, as here with Strimma by alvalinen.de.

DOUBLE TAKE Who says that nesting tables need to stand next to the sofa? This team from nordal.eu also looks great as a unit next to the bed. If you have even less space, just use one.

Brass all over

IN THE AIR Plain, delicate metal baskets can be fixed to the wall to replace bulky bedside cabinets. These two form a particularly nice contrast to the wall colour.

3 COOL TIPS

For gentle unwinding and sweet dreams,
even a small **BEDROOM** can be
transformed into a relaxation centre.

Minimalism

In the bedroom, less is more –
less furniture, less decoration,
fewer patterns and fewer loud
colours. It's the best way
to calm your body and mind.
This rule applies especially in
a tiny home. A room is quickly
overloaded – with furniture as
well as with shapes and objects.
A mix of styles also creates
too much restlessness in the
bedroom. The gaze gets caught
by any number of different
points and is quickly
overwhelmed. If minimalism
prevails in your bedroom,
however, you not only create a
spa-like air of tranquillity, but
also a touch of generous space.

Colours

Dark colours are, of course,
exciting and create fantastic
contrasts. But excitement is
not really a desirable ambience
in the bedroom, and to make a
small room appear more
spacious, light tones are a
better choice anyway. If you
don't want to do without darker
shades, make sure you stay
within one colour family.
For a particularly relaxed
atmosphere, the walls can be
painted in soft grey tones. In
combination with white, the
room will seem lighter and more
open. Furniture and accessories
made from natural materials
bring cosy warmth.

Storage

As anywhere in a tiny home,
the same applies in the
bedroom: order, please!
Everything that's lying around
slows down the gaze and
makes the room appear smaller.
Storage space is a must
in the bedroom, but since bulky
furniture often restricts
movement, it's better to use
light, delicate alternatives
in a small bedroom. An open
hanging shelf makes the area
around the bed appear larger
than a clunky bedside table.
And all the little things that
quickly create an impression
of chaos are simply tidied away
in boxes and baskets.

CHILL OUT
in nature

Carl-Felix is a North German guy whose childhood room had a view of the far distance, and now his tiny holiday home provides spectacular views.

The holiday home measures only 21 sq m (226 sq ft), but the high ceilings make it look spacious and feel open and airy. The skylights admit plenty of sunshine.

The Kaat may look a little futuristic in the middle of a green meadow, but the building materials used to construct it are all natural so it blends in perfectly.

Whether dining or
working, whatever
needs doing can be
done here.

When a carpenter
builds a holiday
home, his material
of choice is of
course wood.
And if, like Carl-Felix, you live near
the coast, your holiday home should
also set the scene with spectacular
views of the sea, the mud flats and
the meadows. The holiday home
in question should perhaps also be
mobile – after all, you might prefer a
different view from your windows at
some point. Carl-Felix also attaches
great importance to an ecological way
of life and construction; he always
keeps the environment and healthy
living in mind when he comes up with
new ideas. And last but not least, the
temporary home should also look cool
and contemporary. Quite a number of
requirements to meet! With the help
of a friend, the resourceful carpenter
set out to put all of them into a very
clever shape. He called his new mobile
tiny home *Kaat* – a Low German word

Sink, refrigerator and two-
burner gas stove – you can
cook on a surprisingly large
scale in a small space.

The lower three steps are hidden under the work surface until they are needed.

The interior wood furnishings not only ensure a modern appearance, they also create a warm and homely feeling as well as a good indoor climate.

The bathroom comprises basin, toilet and shower. It found its place underneath the sleeping level. Here, too, the Scandinavian look dominates, with wood, rough plaster and minimal fittings.

The large Velux window above the sleeping level offers perfect views of the starry night sky. The highlight: the window can be hydraulically opened all the way.

The staircase not only serves as a route to the upper floor, it's also a room divider and sculpture.

meaning something like 'little hut' in translation. That's quite an understatement, because a lot happens in these compact 21 sq m (226 sq ft). In addition to a bathroom and a kitchen, it houses a generously sized bed on its own level, plus a lounge corner with an additional guest bed, a work area and plenty of storage space. And all is presented in a light, Scandinavian-inspired design. Most of the materials are natural – the walls are constructed from modified, impregnated spruce, and the interior and the furniture are also made of spruce. Seaweed is used to ensure good insulation – an obvious choice if you live by the sea. It took a year for all the ideas to be fused into an overall design and structure and for the tiny house with a Scandinavian look to stand on its wheels. In the meantime, the little house has become so popular that Carl-Felix has used the idea to create a business model and he is now also offering his Kaats for sale. ∎

Insights
INTO TINY

HOUSES

Big living in a very small space – the trend towards living in a tiny house indicates that more and more people want to simplify their lives and rid themselves of unnecessary ballast. Those who reduce everything to the bare essentials can often increase the quality of their lives.

Some little houses are mobile and can be moved from one beautiful spot to the next. Others are built to stay in the same place. Some are privately owned homes, others are used as offices, guest accommodation or weekend homes. Still others are rented out as holiday homes. They all have one thing in common: the elegant little houses show that while you may have to forego living space, you don't have to do without comfort. A well-equipped kitchen, a bathroom with a shower, cleverly assigned storage space, a cosy seating area and a large bed, often on a second level – that's all you need to live comfortably.

The decision to choose a tiny house is based not only on idealism, but also on your finances. Of course, a home that measures only 25 sq m (270 sq ft) will be much cheaper than one that extends over 120 sq m (1,292 sq ft). A plot of land can be bought or leased, but this too costs money. Sometimes a tiny house is just a stopover, a temporary home in one place before moving on to the next.

If you are thinking of minimizing your living space, why not rent a tiny holiday house for a weekend or an entire holiday break before making your decision? Does it give you an all-round good feeling? Then nothing stands in the way of moving. ∎

TINY
HOUSE
No 1

The kitchenette is small, but it has all the features you need. Thanks to its handleless fronts, it sits perfectly in the room.

A large mirror generates a feeling of spaciousness in a small bathroom.

With its dark spruce wood façade, this tiny house blends in perfectly with its natural surroundings.

Well positioned

CABIN-ONE.COM How much space do you need? Two people can live well in a Cabin One. If you require more space it expands to Cabin Bay, and the Cabin Suite can even accommodate four people. All share a minimalist design. Clear lines, lots of wood inside and out, and an extravagant shape are the hallmarks of these cabins. Particularly practical is the fact that you can live in one on a trial basis before making the decision to buy.

NAME Cabin One, a tiny house for two

SIZE 28 sq m (300 sq ft) usable area

BEST FEATURE The huge gable window which floods the interior with light and also guarantees magnificent views.

Falling asleep under a starry sky and being roused by the rays of the sun – a skylight makes it possible.

Just like the large panoramic window, the bench extends along the entire gable end. There's plenty of storage space hidden under the seat.

TINY HOUSE No 2

The red roof and door provide a happy glow in what is otherwise rather reserved in terms of colour. In the Manteo home, a combination of white and stained wood sets the tone. The windows are small, but still let in plenty of light.

Home on wheels

MODERNTINYLIVING.COM A passion for an adventurous life and solid craftsmanship brought together friends in Columbus, Ohio. Their objective is to build the most beautiful, safest, most roadworthy and most modern tiny houses. Their catalogue includes different model series, but they also accommodate customers' individual design wishes.

NAME Manteo (based on The Point model), a holiday home for four persons

SIZE 22 sq m (237 sq ft)

BEST FEATURE The antiqued floor, which exudes a very special ambience. The white walls and ceilings are visually neutral and backgrounded, giving the limelight to the floor and allowing it to become the star of the show.

You'll sleep like
a king or queen
on the upper level,
and the sitting area
below converts
into a second
bedroom.

Wardrobe under the stairs –
every corner in the tiny
house has its use.

The bathroom is opposite
the kitchenette, behind
sliding doors. Everything
here is compact and
cleverly designed.

Gleaming white combined with dark wood and soft greys create a comfortable country house ambience.

Food with a view – the breakfast bar is directly adjacent to the kitchen. And you could just as easily open up your laptop here and set up your home office.

TINY HOUSE No 3

Thanks to the windows and the white walls, the raised sleeping level does not feel cramped at all.

Very stylish

MINTTINYHOMES.COM The Canadian Mint Tiny House Company has been supplying fans of living in small places with various house models since 2014. Their main customer base is in Canada as well as the United States. The environment is very important to the company – so it's quite appropriate that living in a tiny home significantly reduces the residents' carbon footprint.

NAME Aero Edition

SIZE 22 sq m (237 sq ft)

BEST FEATURE The skylight above the bed, which, together with the two windows, lets you fall asleep while gazing at the stars.

One of the smaller models, the Aero Edition is a particularly versatile tiny house – both on the roads and while looking for a plot of land.

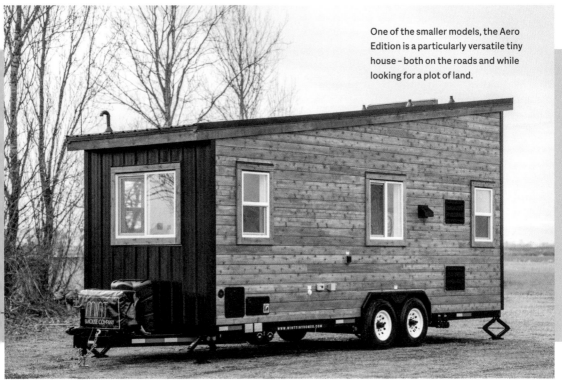

Eating and working next to the washing machine – the wooden panelling makes it hardly noticeable.

All the way along – from the sofa at one end you can see all the way through to the kitchen, the sleeping area and the back wall of the shower.

TINY HOUSE No 4

Feel welcome to stay. The floral windowboxes and the lattice windows look exceptionally inviting.

The marble washbasin and the black base unit make this bathroom feel classy.

You only need to rearrange the cushions and the sofa morphs into a guest bed, with plenty of storage space underneath.

Country living

MODERNTINYLIVING.COM Can't find anything totally suitable among the standard models of small homes? No problem, the company will also build tailor-made tiny houses, such as this one. The elegant blue kitchen featuring a narrow counter and bar stools opposite the units is particularly successful. The gable roof and the plants on the façade give the house a true country feel.

NAME Allswell (made to measure)

SIZE 22 sq m (237 sq ft)

BEST FEATURE The floor-to-ceiling windows in the sleeping area, which can be opened like garage doors at the push of a button.

Minimalist

VIPP.COM This tiny house is ready to welcome people looking for relaxation in the Swedish forests. Huge windows bring forest and water directly into the holiday home. This wonderful combination of modern architecture and untouched nature is manufactured and rented to holidaymakers by Danish company Vipp.

NAME Shelter, holiday home for two

SIZE 55 sq m (592 sq ft)

BEST FEATURE The view of the lake and the forest right outside the door.

This sleeping alcove promises serious relaxation and sweet dreams.

The black cuboid home blends surprisingly well with its natural setting.

The sliding doors blur the boundaries between inside and outside. The black interior looks extravagant, but not gloomy.

TINY HOUSE No 5

The house is fully equipped with Vipp furniture and accessories, from the rubbish bin to the kitchen cupboards.

TINY HOUSE No 6

Straight from the bed into the lake – not a problem here.

The bright and friendly decor makes this tiny house seem more spacious.

Brushing your teeth with a view – instead of looking into the mirror, the view is of the greenery outside.

The porthole leaves no doubt about the location on the lake shore.

The loft is secured with nets against the risk of falling and for a maritime flair. The airy ladder can be pushed out of the way.

Holiday feel

SEEDATSCHEN.DE A *dacha* is a piece of land with a weekend house, so Seedatschen is the perfect name for a company that rents holiday homes on the edge of Hainer Lake in Germany. There are three sizes to choose from – their version of a tiny house accommodates two people.

NAME Zweiufer

SIZE 14 sq m (151 sq ft)

BEST FEATURE The workshop stove, which creates a great cosy atmosphere even when the weather is lousy and you're stuck inside.

TINY
HOUSE
No 7

This tiny house offers plenty of living space over just 6 m (20 ft) in length.

The generously spacious living room conceals lots of storage space, not only underneath the benches but also below the raised floor.

Even the stairs can hide a multitude of important and trivial items.

totally natural

MODERNTINYLIVING.COM You will feel right up close to nature in a Sage Point, not only thanks to its wooden cladding on the outside – its interior is also reminiscent of a lodge in the middle of a forest. The cupboard fronts are painted in sage green, so they harmonize perfectly with the grain of the interior cladding. This tiny house has two sleeping areas: a raised level above the kitchen as well as a bathroom and a seating area that can be converted into a bed at the other end of the house.

NAME Sage Point (a version of the The Point model)

SIZE 22 sq m (237 sq ft)

BEST FEATURE The additional storage space hidden under the floor of the living room.

From your bed you can appreciate the green spaces outside on three sides.

The tiny home offers a harmonious blend of colours and materials, from the living room to the mini-bathroom behind the sliding door.

TINY HOUSE No 8

The Mohican is completely clad in pine and cedar wood. The interior also features varnished wood and matches the outer shell. An elegant choice for nature-lovers, but also for everyone who likes things straightforward.

Two floors

MODERNTINYLIVING.COM This model is known as The Mohican. Without any frills, its strong points are the clear lines, compact shape and solid construction. The tiny house can easily be moved from one place to another, so it also makes an ideal mobile holiday home, but of course you may wish to find a more permanent position for it.

NAME The Mohican

SIZE Ground floor: 15 sq m (161 sq ft), loft 6.5 sq m (70 sq ft)

BEST FEATURE The many windows and the glass-fronted door, which allow the light to flood the entire mini-house unhindered.

Black metal creates a touch of industrial style and spices up the white living area.

The stained maple wood introduces warmth and comfort to the house.

All belongings are hidden behind closed fronts. There is space for books and other treasures on the open shelf.

> *Living with flexible storage solutions*

Suppliers, manufacturers & information

LIGHTING

andtradition.com
ayilluminate.com
flos.com
himmee.com
hkliving.nl
innolux.fi
lampegras.fr
lightyears.dk
louispoulsen.com
muuto.com
northernlighting.no
superliving.dk
tomdixon.net
wastberg.com

INTERIORS AND ACCESSORIES

affari.nu
alki.fr
ambientedirect.com
avocadostore.de
blomus.com
bloomingville.com
bungalow.dk
bywirth.com
carlhansen.com
car-moebel.de
connox.de
estampille52.fr
fdbmobler.dk
fermliving.de
framacph.com
greenliving-shop.de
grueneerde.com
hartodesign.fr
hay.dk
hemashop.com
hessnatur.com
housedoctor.com
hubsch-interior.com
iblaursen.dk
ikarus.de
impressionen.de
karakter-copenhagen.com
korbo.se

lenebjerre.com
liv-interior.com
magisdesign.com
manufactum.de
moebe.dk
naturehome.com
nordal.eu
normann-copenhagen.com
norsu.com.au
richard lampert
roije.com
sidebyside-shop.com
skagerak.dk
sostrenegrene.com
stilconceptstore.de
stringfurniture.com
treku.com
wayfair.de
westwingnow.de

MODULAR FURNITURE

ambivalenz.org
cubit-shop.com
made.com
muellermoebel.de
mycs.com
pickawood.com
stocubo.de
usm.com

MODULAR KITCHENS

bloc-modulkuechen.de
bulthaup.com
bycocoon.com
cane-line.de
framacph.com
home24.de
ikea.com
miniki.eu
naber.de
roshults.com
siematic.com
stadtnomaden.com
steel-cucine.com
tomas-kitchen-living.co.uk

SLEEPING

alvalinen.de
auping.com
bettenrid.de
brunobett.de
flexform.it
magazin.com
schlaraffia.de
smartbett.de
swisssense.de

HOLIDAY HOMES

hofgut.info
klitzeklein.org
naturama-beilngries.de
naturhaeuschen.de
pier9-hotel.de
puresleben.at
seedatschen.de
tinyescape.de

TINY HOUSES

addaroom.dk
cabin-one.com
extrahuset.se
gotiny.de
greentinyhouses.com
kleinernomade.org
meyers-tiny-house.de
minttinyhomes.com
moderntinyliving.com
mycubig.com
rolling-tiny-house.de
tiny-house-diekmann.de
vipp.com
wohnwagon.at
wood-cube.com

INFO

thetinylife.com
tinyhomebuilders.com
tinyhouse.com
tinyhouselistings.com
tiny-house.info
tiny-house-helden.de
tiny-houses.de

Marion Hellweg

lives in Munich with her daughter, Florentine. A trained carpenter, restorer and interior designer, she was for many years editor-in-chief of the magazines *House & Gardening* and *Wohnträume*, as well as publisher and editor-in-chief of the Scandinavian interiors magazines *Sweet Living Magazin* and *My Homestyle*. Marion is now editor-in-chief of the interior and lifestyle magazine *Living & More*. In 2011 she set up her own company, *Nord Liv*, as a freelance journalist, editor, stylist and interior designer and established herself as a successful book author in the areas of architecture, interiors and lifestyle.

Frederike Treu

lives with her sons, husband and animals in Worpswede in northern Germany. A cultural studies expert, she started her own business as a freelance journalist in 2009 after occupying various positions in publishing houses and agencies. Since then, she has written mainly about her two great passions – lifestyle and gardens. Her features, columns and reviews are published in magazines such as *Living & More*, *Living at Home*, *GartenFlora*, *Cosmopolitan* and *Laura*.

Thanks

A big thank you goes to Frederike – without your word-perfect
support, this book would not have been possible!
I would like to thank all the photographers, picture agencies,
manufacturers and companies who provided us with their
inspirational images for this book. I would also like to thank Florentine
and my family and friends for their love and support.
And last but not least: a heartfelt 'Merci!' to the entire Prestel team
for their excellent teamwork. I would particularly like to thank
Julie Kiefer for her confidence and commitment and Sabine Loos for her
wonderful layout – a creative collaboration couldn't work any better.

Picture credits

p2: Christina Kayser O. / Living Inside; p4: House Doctor;
p5: SARIPICTURE, Sarah Domandl; p6: Marc Heldens, Kaschkasch;
p7: Moebe, Cabin One; pp8-9: SieMatic; p11: Ikea; p12:
INT2architecture; pp14-23: Natalie Spadavecchia, The Palm Co;
p24: H&M Home; p25: House Doctor; p26: House Doctor; p27:
Ikea, Cabin One, see manufacturers; p28: Ikea, see manufacturers;
pp30-41: INT2architecture; p42: INT2architecture; p43:
INT2architecture; p44: Paola Bagna: Ringo Paulusch, Vania da Rui,
see manufacturers; p45: Ikea; p46: Vipp, Car Möbel; pp48-57:
Greg Cox / bureaux.co.za; pp58-59: see manufacturers; p60:
Ambivalenz; p61: String; p62: see manufacturers; pp64-71: Marc
Heldens; p72: House Doctor; p73: Vipp, Sp74: House Doctor; p75:
Stadtnomaden, SieMatic; p76: bureaux.co.za, see manufacturers;
pp78-83: Michael K Chen Architecture, Alan Tansey; p84: House
Doctor; p85: INT2architecture; p86: Avenue Lifestyle, Holly
Marder, Velux, see manufacturers; p87: Ikea; p88: Bezmirno,
Ikea; p89: n by Naber; pp90-91: Ikea; p92: bureaux.co.za;
pp94-103: Christina Kayser O. / Living Inside; p104: Korbo;
p105: Bungalow; pp106-107: see manufacturers, Car Möbel;
p108: Alvhem, see manufacturers; p109: Car Möbel; p110: House
Doctor, see manufacturers; pp111-119: Nicholay Gurney, Katherine
Lu, Michael Wee; p120: bureaux.co.za; p121: Schlaraffia;
p122: FDB Møbler, see manufacturers; p123: Moebe;
pp124-125: INT2architecture, see manufacturers; p126: see
manufacturers; pp128-135: Warren Heath / bureaux.co.za;
p136: Müller Möbelwerkstätten; p137: House Doctor;
p138: Moebe, see manufacturers; p139: Ikea; p140: House
Doctor, see manufacturers; pp142-145: kaschkasch;
pp146-151: Marc Heldens; pp152-153: Ikea; p154: Frama, see
manufacturers; p155: String; p156: Vipp; p157: Ikea,
see manufacturers; p158: Ikea, see manufacturers; pp159-167:
Pauline Legoff; p168: Bloomingville; p169: House Doctor; p170:
House Doctor; p171: see manufacturers, Portrait: Sylwia Gervais;
p172: see manufacturers; p173: Ikea; p174: see manufacturers;
pp176-181: House Doctor, add a room; p182: INT2architecture;
p183: Vipp; p184: String; p185: Müller Möbelwerkstätten;
p186: Oyoy, see manufacturers; p187: Alvhem; S. Nordal,
see manufacturers; pp188-197; Kaat; pp198-199: see
manufacturers; pp200-201: Cabin One; pp202-203: Modern Tiny
Living; pp204-205: Mint Tiny Homes; pp206-207: Modern Tiny
Living; pp208-209: Vipp; pp210-211: Seedatschen;
pp212-213: Modern Tiny Living; pp214-215: Modern Tiny Living;
pp216-217: Treku; p219: Velux; p220: Portrait Marion Hellweg:
Sylwia Gervais, Portrait Frederike Treu: Ingo Jagels;
pp220-221: Treku; p222: Car Möbel; p224: Pauline Legoff

© Prestel Verlag, Munich · London · New York, 2021
A member of Penguin Random House Verlagsgruppe GmbH
Neumarkter Strasse 28 · 81673 Munich

Library of Congress Control Number is available; a CIP catalogue record for this book is available from the British Library.

Idea and concept Marion Hellweg, marionhellweg.com
Texts Frederike Treu
Editorial direction Julie Kiefer
Project management, translation and typesetting Sylvia Goulding
Editor Mike Goulding
Proofreader Diana Vowles
Design and layout Sabine Loos, Berlin
Cover image Greg Cox/bureaux.co.za
Back cover images Natalie Spadavecchia/The Palm Co, Marc Heldens, Modern Tiny Living
Production management Andrea Cobré
Separations Schnieber Graphik GmbH, Munich
Printing and binding DZS GRAFIK, d.o.o.
Paper Magno Natural

MIX
Paper from responsible sources
FSC® C106600

Penguin Random House Verlagsgruppe FSC® N001967

Climate neutral
Print product
ClimatePartner.com/14044-1912-1001

Printed in Slovenia

ISBN 978-3-7913-8761-1

www.prestel.com